Creating Fresh Images for Preaching

N₀

Creating Fresh Images for Preaching

THOMAS H. TROEGER

New Rungs for Jacob's Ladder

MORE EFFECTIVE PREACHING SERIES

Judson Press ® Valley Forge

CREATING FRESH IMAGES FOR PREACHING
Copyright © 1982
Judson Press, Valley Forge, PA 19481

Unless otherwise indicated, the Scripture quotations in this publication are from the Revised Standard Version of the Bible copyrighted 1946, 1952 © 1971, 1973 by the Division of Christian Education of the National Council of the Churches of Christ in the U.S.A., and used by permission.

Other quotations of the Bible are from *The New Testament in Modern English,* rev. ed. Copyright © J. B. Phillips 1972. Used by permission of The Macmillan Company and Geoffrey Bles, Ltd.

Excerpts from FOUR QUARTETS by T. S. Eliot are reprinted by permission of Harcourt Brace Jovanovich, Inc.; copyright 1943 by T. S. Eliot; renewed 1971 by Esme Valerie Eliot.

The quotes from *Genesis, a Commentary* by Gerhard von Rad: Copyright © MCMLXI, W. L. Jenkins. © SCM Press, Ltd., 1972. Used by permission of The Westminster Press.

Quotes from *Collected Poems* by Conrad Aiken: Copyright © 1953, 1970 by Conrad Aiken; renewed 1981 by Mary Aiken. Reprinted by permission of Oxford University Press, Inc.

Library of Congress Cataloging in Publication Data

Troeger, Thomas H., 1945–
    Creating fresh images for preaching.

    1. Preaching. I. Title.
BV4211.2.T76   251   81-13674
ISBN 0-8170-0937-X   AACR2

The name JUDSON PRESS is registered as a trademark in the U.S. Patent Office.

Printed in the U.S.A. ⊕

For

Chester
Clancey
Don
Miriam
Paul
Rosalie

Contents

Prelude: Visions and Voices

It is Tuesday afternoon and you are riding home from a pastoral call. But it is not the conversation with your parishioner that occupies your thoughts. A single question snags your mind: *What shall I preach about on Sunday?* You flit from one idea to the next. When you arrive at your office, you leaf through a file of ideas or skim through some books in which you have marked passages that struck you with their power of thought and expression. Or maybe you recall a news story or an issue in your own community that seems to require a word from the pulpit. Still nothing clicks. Perhaps you are using the lectionary, but when you read the lessons for Sunday, the words seem nothing more than ancient dust. Even the commentaries do not bring them alive. That evening at a meeting your attention wanders from the agenda back to the question: *What shall I preach about on Sunday?*

The fact that you are struggling is not a sign that you are inadequate as a preacher. If you were never perplexed about what to preach, it might indicate that your preaching has fallen into a predictable pattern that makes for easy preparation but dull listening. And it would suggest that you have lost a sense of the audacity of the task: a human being trying to speak for God.

But sometimes perplexity becomes paralysis. After repeated efforts at settling on a passage or a theme, you find yourself stumped. The next morning you can squeeze out a title for the bulletin, but the subject is lead in your heart.

If only the hollow air of your study would thicken with the blaze and smoke of the divine presence the way it happens in the Bible:

Holiness overwhelms Isaiah.
Fire burns in Jeremiah's bones.
A heavenly host sings to shepherds.
Wind and flame rush among the apostles.
Light dazzles Paul.

But no angels visit you, and heaven does not open to reveal Sunday's message. You sit in your study remembering that you need to order ink for the mimeograph machine, and you begin to dial Arlot's Office Supply. Wait a minute.

Visions and voices.

Do not give up on them so soon. Human activity is no substitute for divine action. You and I know that. How many times have we preached that to our people? Yet here we are, trying the very strategy that we have declared will not work. If workaholic business people won't find salvation through their busyness, why should preachers?

> Isaiah's temple vision better suits
> an age of quieter piety than ours.
> Our temples are too busy doing the work
> of temples; much too noisy in the task
> of making temple sounds. Our temples temple.
> From morning until night, frenetically,
> they go about the busy work of templing.
> We haven't anything against Isaiah.
> It's only that we've got a *thing* with temples.[1]

Of course, the mimeograph machine won't print the bulletin without being refilled. But what is supposed to be flowing through the church: ink or Spirit? ". . . the written code kills, but the Spirit gives life" (2 Corinthians 3:6). Paul wrote that in another context, but it applies here as well. A Sunday bulletin in clear, bold print with no smudges and a sermon manuscript without "typos" cannot replace the impassioned word, the word charged with conviction, the word of one who has touched holy things.

Visions and voices.

You flip through the pages of the commentaries and the Bible dictionaries spread out on your desk from yesterday's barren search and decide you better get down to work. Maybe the psalmist could afford to wait on the Lord like watchmen craning their necks for the dawn, but the secretary goes home at 2:30 and the rest of the week is one long meeting. All watchmen keep watching; the preacher has got to preach.

You write the first sentence: "This morning's text is about.
. . ." Finally, a vision: Andrea Winston's husband is leaning
against the wall under the Sarah Barnes Noble memorial window
with his eyes shut and Margaret Linden has handed her son,
Peter, a pencil with which to draw on the bulletin.

Next comes a voice, not from heaven but from the secretary's
desk. "If you give me the announcements, I can type up the
stencil for the back sheet."

> From morning until night, frenetically,
> we celebrate the work of cerebration.
> We do not want to listen and respond.
> We want to take command. We want to work,
> manipulate, and cerebrate the Word.
> In any case, the *hearing* of the Word
> comes hard for us. . . .[2]

The hearing of the Word—and the seeing, too!—does come hard
for us. How do you, the preacher, hear the Word? How do you
see the Word? And by "Word" I do not just mean the thousand-
odd pages from Genesis through Revelation that are bound in
black and lying on the desk next to the pew cards that the ushers
pulled from the collection plate. I mean the Word who forges
your bones and hinges your hands and crochets the net of
capillaries that feeds your body. I mean the power behind the
force that unfurls the flower from the bud and pumps from the
center of a bruised heart the words "I forgive you." There is no
book that makes that Word plainer than the Bible, but the Bible
is not itself that Word. If it were, John would have written: "In
the beginning was the Bible, and the Bible was with God, and
the Bible was God. . . . And the Bible became flesh and dwelt
among us, full of grace and truth. . . ." (cf. John 1:1, 14).

How, then, do you see and hear the breathing Word to which
the typeset words in your Bible point? Concordances, commentaries, lexicons, parallel translations—all may help you; yet in
themselves they are not enough. There is a flame that must
illumine the eye and a whisper that must flutter against the ear
to make our faith dance inside us, to animate our preaching
with energy and grace, to use our fragile, fading human words
as vessels of the eternal Word.

Visions and voices.

You pick up one of the pew cards on your desk. The box next
to "I would like the pastor to call" is checked, and scribbled in
the margin is an urgent message: "This week, *please!*" This week,

this day, this hour, this minute, this second. Who has time for visions and voices? Mystics and dreamers and the Center for Holistic Living located down the street. But name one minister, squeezed by the world, who ever had time for visions and voices.

"But so much more the report went abroad concerning him; and great multitudes gathered to hear and to be healed of their infirmities. But he withdrew to the wilderness and prayed" (Luke 5:1-16).

It takes discipline to see and to hear the visions and voices of God in our life, discipline every bit as strenuous as exegesis. There is a sharpening of the eye and a training of the ear that can help us avoid mistaking the hollowness of our study for the absence of the Spirit.

Art students in a still-life class learn that the image on the retina offers more riches than the brain can catalogue or the hand can draw. The instructor arranges a vase and three oranges. Behind this arrangement light slants in through a paned window. The students record what they see: a vase and three oranges. Then the instructor asks: "What about the shadow thrown by the first orange on the second and the second on the third? Have you noticed the relationship between the fruit and the circle pattern at the neck of the vase? Observe the tinge of citrus color reflected in the glaze of the base." Light and shadow, texture and shape, color and line create a universe whose subtleties elude the unalerted eye—as do visions and voices the unexpectant soul.

This book trains the preacher's eye to trace the play of heaven's light upon earth's shadowed surface, and it tunes the preacher's ear to hear the overtones of grace that sound in human speech.

The reality of God surrounds us; the dynamics of that deep mystery of our life and our world is at hand with every breeze and breath. It is true, we are not always aware of it, due to our propensity for looking on our own ways and being concerned for others and for the creatures and things of the world primarily insofar [as] they may be useful to our purposes. Isn't that largely what is called the secular aspect of life? In getting intrigued by utility and the profitable, we tend to suppress the awareness of mystery and the sense of wonder in our life. Thus we need being reminded. We need some messenger, some angel of God to remind us—just as it happened to Moses. The rumor of angels, to be sure, is resounding throughout the universe, but we usually don't listen. It takes an angel to be sent specifically to you, when your awareness has subsided or become dull.[3]

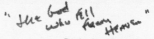
"the God who fell from Heaven"

The air is thicker with the divine presence than first we realized. But who will believe our witness that God is with us if our voices lack the conviction of experience? We preachers cannot tell our people to be alive to the Spirit unless we ourselves are. It is presumptuous to figure out how we will communicate in a sermon when we leave unexamined how God is communicating with us. Perhaps the stillness in our study is telling us not to speak on behalf of heaven's court until we have listened to the King:

> We say amiss,
> This or that is;
> Thy word is all, if we could spell.[4]

How will we "spell" the Word? How will we arrange the syllables of existence—the stories, images, and issues of life and Scripture—so that people can recognize the Word in their daily experience?

Spelling the Word requires seeing and hearing the Word. So before we order ink for the mimeograph machine or stack the pew cards in our pocket calendar for the afternoon's calls, let us open ourselves to visions and voices from the truth we would proclaim.

open self to visions + voices

Visions of God

Two disciples are lugging Jesus' body into the tomb. One disciple has wrapped his arms around Jesus' torso from behind. The other is carrying him by his legs. A third disciple looks on in desperation while his companions haul the yellowed, pain-shriveled body of their friend into a hollow rock.

That is how the German expressionist Emil Nolde pictures the burial of Jesus in his painting *The Entombment*. I had just hung a full-color reproduction of the work in my office when a woman came by to see me about some other matter and said, "I wish you'd take that picture down. It's awful."

"Why?"

"Because it makes Jesus look so dead. If you want a Good Friday picture of Jesus, you should get a photograph of Michelangelo's *Pieta*. I saw a picture of it in St. Monica's Hospital. It was over my bed after my operation and it made Jesus seem very close. It shows Jesus as smooth-skinned and athletic."

"Crucified, dead, and buried." The ancient words filed into my head like a procession of monks. "Crucified, dead, and buried." They are words that generation after generation has spoken, words that people have fought about and rebelled against, words that this woman has repeated Sunday after Sunday for nearly sixty years. The picture "makes Jesus look so dead" she said. Well, don't the words do the same? "Crucified, dead, and buried." Dead is dead. Buried is buried. Words mean what they say. Don't they?

Evidently not. Words mean what we see, not what they say. For me the words "crucified, dead, and buried" call up Nolde's picture of a yellowed, pain-shriveled body. For the woman they awaken Michelangelo's smooth-skinned, athletic Jesus. For Isabel Moore, the central character of *Final Payments*, "crucified, dead, and buried" means a church on Good Friday and the memory of her father's death and the anxiety of her own:

> The church was dark with the number of the congregation. And the statues, covered in their purple cloth, stole what light there would have been available. A sense of unaccustomed shock hung in the air, as if the people kneeling here this afternoon were waiting for a storm. I too knelt and put my hands in front of my face. I thought of Christ, of the death of Christ. We were here to acknowledge the presence of death among us. We were here to acknowledge our own inevitable deaths.
>
> My father was dead; there was the pain. I had loved him, but my love had not been able to help him. Even my love had not made him immune. I had wanted to inject him with love like a vaccine, to keep him from loss as you might keep a town from cholera. But my love had not kept him from death, had not even held back the impulse of his brain that shattered and destroyed his nerves even as I stood near him. Love had kept nothing back; not even the smallest disasters. My father had died, but I had not killed him, as I had not been able to save him. I would die; everyone in this church would die. Everyone I knew and loved would die. . . .[1]

"Crucified, dead, and buried." Four plain words. Three adjectives and a conjunction. The perfect outline for a three-point sermon for Holy Week. It sounds so easy until you step into the pulpit and you look out and realize who is sitting in the congregation. Isabel Moore is there grieving for her father. You can see it in the shadow in her eyes. The old woman is looking away from you and waiting for the smooth-skinned, athletic Jesus to float in marbled smoothness from your lips. And others are there imagining the pain-shriveled body of Jesus or the wasted figure of someone they loved.

"Crucified, dead, and buried." Four plain words?

No.

Words are never plain, least of all the words of faith. They are more like wells into depths and mineshafts in bedrock. Follow them. Follow them down deep because they will lead you to the center of the human heart where God's visions are seen.

"Crucified, dead, and buried."

Do not assume that the clear grammatical sense of the words is what will flash in the mind's eye of the listener. Reach your way into the meaning of the words by grabbing hold of the images that they awaken. Use the visual associations as a banister to hold onto as you descend into the text:

> For God alone my soul waits in silence;
>   from him comes my salvation.
> He only is my rock and my salvation,
>   my fortress; I shall not be greatly moved.
>   —Psalm 62:1-2

Stop. What do you see?

Perhaps nothing. That is usually the case when preachers first try this exercise. They are thinking too hard about the "sense of the text," about the writer's doctrine of God, about what they will tell the congregation, about illustrations and applications.

Read the text again:

> For God alone my soul waits in silence;
>   from him comes my salvation.
> He only is my rock and my salvation,
>   my fortress; I shall not be greatly moved.

Stop. What do you see?

A rock.

Yes, a rock! God is a rock. That is what the psalmist says. You scribble down your theme, "God is utterly dependable."

No. Don't do this. It will cut off the visual associations too soon in the creative process. Do not go back to the purely verbal and abstract. Follow down deeper the associations of rock. If God is a rock, then what is God not?

God is not an idea.

God is not a feeling.

God is not an experience.

God is not a proposition.

God IS a rock.

What's a rock like?

Solid. Dependable. Enduring.

Why would I want a rock?

Stability. Everything else is shifting and sinking: values and institutions, customs and traditions, beliefs and loyalties. All are changing. Nothing is still. But God is a rock.

What can I do with a rock?

You can stand on a rock. Stand for justice. Stand for truth. You can build on a rock. Build community. Build character. You can use a rock for a cornerstone. The cornerstone of our life and our salvation.

Give me the rock!

Go back again to the commentaries. Trace out that word "rock" with a concordance. Find out how it is used in different contexts. What were the historical circumstances that made Israel want God to be its rock? You may even want to look through an illustrated Bible atlas and get pictures of rocks and cliffs securely in your mind. Your visual probing of the word will give your scholarly pursuits a vividness and urgency that they may have lacked before.

When you preach the sermon, do not bury the rock under a mudslide of concepts. Yes, explore the complexities of the text and your congregation's life, but remember how the image "rock" made your sermon preparation take fire. If God communicates with you through an image, then that tells you something about how to let God speak through you to the congregation. Share the vision you received! God is a rock. That is the psalmist's vision. God is a rock. That has become your vision. God is a rock. That can be your people's vision. The rock will give coherence and clarity to the subtleties of your sermon. Repeat the image. God is a rock. Drive it home. God is a rock. Let people feel the solidness of God. Trust God in your preaching. Trust the message you are preaching. If God is a rock and if you can get your people to stand on God, then they are not going to sink. Develop the image, and let the image take over when you sit down. If Isabel Moore finally stands on the rock, she may find peace about her father's death and power to face the future death of her friends and herself. If that woman who wants the smooth-skinned, athletic Jesus feels God the rock beneath her feet, she may be able to acknowledge the Suffering Servant who had no comeliness or beauty and who was wounded for our transgressions. Give Isabel and the old woman the rock, and the rock will hold them up. After all, that is what the psalmist says: "He only is my rock and my salvation, my fortress; I shall not be greatly moved."

"Crucified, dead, and buried."

"He only is my rock."

They are nothing but words; yet they are more than words: images. "The Bible is the greatest treasure-house of powerful, disturbing, life-enhancing images in the whole of humanity's long history."[2] If we preachers are going to be scribes trained for the kingdom who can bring out of our treasure-house what is new and what is old (Matthew 13:52), then we need to understand that the images of faith are like all great visions and symbols.

Great symbols swallow us whole. They lead us on into themselves . . . we pursue . . . but we never capture their whole meaning. Not because the symbol is mindlessly obscure (though there are literary vices of this kind too) but because it is radically, authentically enignmatic. The figures of Prospero, Ariel, and Caliban, or Beethoven's sixteenth quartet, or Rembrandt's painting of the old woman paring her nails are supreme symbols because they draw the mind beyond its limit. We might talk, argue, and analyze all our lives, but never exhaust their meaning; they can never be replaced by summary or interpretation. The artist has given us something absolute and irreducible. At last, such symbols survive in their own being as the only possible way of saying what they say. What Archibald MacLeish once said of poetry may be said of the symbol. A symbol "must not mean but be."[3]

And a sermon must not mean but be! That is a dangerous idea. It could become an excuse for sloppy preaching, that meanders aimlessly, vibrating the molecules of space in the sanctuary but never touching the nerve endings of the congregation.

Yes, that is a danger. "A sermon must not mean but be" sounds like the excuse that a clever preaching student might come up with when the class says it could not follow what was being said. But there are more cures for incoherence than logic. Instead of depending on meaning, a preacher can glue a sermon together through the being of an image or story. A repeated phrase or a vision can hold the preacher's words together even as "crucified, dead, and buried" and "rock" hold together what I am writing. The image provides a visual focus around which listeners can arrange not only the preacher's thoughts but also their own life and experience. The preacher's words are like particles of truth placed in the air to crystalize as visions of meaning in the congregation.

"You'll never know what the sermon meant to me today, Pastor." That common response at the door after the service is true for every listener engaged by what we say. Our words are hooking images and meanings that we will never know.

Whose Bog Are We Talking About?

"God is a rock." The theme of Reverend Frazer's semon was buzzing in his head when he entered the church from the door behind the piano and sat down in a high-backed Victorian chair with a worn, purple velvet seat. There was one new face in the small congregation, a boy about eight sitting next to Bud and Lottie Trusdale. *Must be their grandson*, thought Reverend Frazer. *He's got his mother's face—oval, like an egg, with skin tight as a shell—and big eyes.*

Peter Linden did not know the pastor was looking at him. Peter picked up a fan from the hymn rack and waved it hard to try to keep himself awake before the service began. The air conditioner was on the blink, and someone had rounded up the old fans from a closet in the church school hall. Peter was still groggy from the train trip, getting into Lexington late the night before, and riding down to his grandparents' farm. Peter stopped and inspected the fan more closely. It was a stiff piece of cardboard cut in the shape of the entrance to a train tunnel and had a tongue depressor stapled to it for a handle. On one side was a picture of Jesus dressed in a maroon velour bathrobe knocking on somebody's door at night. The sky was midnight blue with a crescent moon that was the same pale gold as Jesus' hands and face, as though his body were molded from the missing substance of a full moon. Curving around the margin of the picture were the words "I stand at the door and knock." The other side of the fan read:

STEVENS' FUNERAL HOME
Serving the Shihabi River Valley for Fifty Years

The thought of fishing in the river that afternoon with his grandfather lifted Peter's sleep spirits so that he was quite awake when the congregation sang its opening hymn, "Holy, Holy, Holy," and the choir processed in.

At the end of the hymn members of the congregation sat down and started fanning themselves while the minister read the Scripture lessons. Peter noticed that not all of the fans had Jesus knocking at the door. The fan the woman in front of him was holding had Jesus in the same bathrobe, but he was carrying a lamb in one arm and holding a shepherd's crook in the other. The woman stopped fanning for a minute and Peter could read "The Lord is my Shepherd." Peter shifted in the pew to see around the other side of the woman's head. He wanted to know if the fan said "STEVENS' FUNERAL HOME."

KEPLER'S INSURANCE AGENCY
Peace of Mind Is Our Business

His grandfather put his arm around Peter's shoulder and made him straighten up. Reverend Frazer was starting his sermon.

"God is a rock. God is a rock. That is what the psalmist tells us." The preacher declared his theme twice. "You can stand on a rock; a rock doesn't give way. When I go hunting down in the swamp off Millcroft Road, I go tramping through a lot of muck."

Peter pictured the bog he played in back home. He pretended he was walking through the muck in his bare feet. Slurp, whack, slurp, whack, slurp, whack.

"But there is a rock in the swamp where I can stand with my gun, and I don't worry about sinking at all." The edge in Reverend Frazer's voice cut through Peter's daydream. "God is like that rock. Life can be a swamp. It can swallow us up unless we stand on the rock. God is that rock. There's a rock and there's a swamp, and you must decide where you are going to stand.

"Drinking is a swamp. I once knew a miner named Cedric Ohlman. He was one of the best miners this area had ever seen when coal was big here. He made excellent money. Everyone wanted Cedric to work for them. Then he started to drink. He drank Friday and he drank Saturday. Sometimes he would come to church with his eyes the color of a spring salamander. Soon his wife and kids left him and he was found drunk and drowned in the Shihabi River."

Peter noticed his grandparents shaking their heads like they knew the story themselves.

"Drink is a swamp, but God is the rock."

Peter leaned against his grandmother and shut his eyes. He imagined his bog with a big, solid rock in the middle. He walked out toward the rock through the muck. Slurp, whack, slurp, whack, slurp, whack. But he did not seem to be getting any closer to the rock. A woman appeared on the rock who was fanning herself. STEVENS' FUNERAL HOME. Peter could see Jesus' hands and face and the crescent moon. A shadowy figure sat down on the moon and played "Holy, Holy, Holy." Someone started to put an extension ladder from the rock to the moon. Peter tried walking faster toward the rock; but the more energy he put out, the more he sank into the bog. Then Peter heard the preacher ending his sermon.

"God is my rock. God is your rock. God is our rock. Stand on the rock and you will never drown in the swamp."

They took the offering while the choir sang an anthem and members of the congregation paddled the damp air with their fans. Then came prayers, and they sang a closing hymn that Peter hardly heard because he was trying to figure out how he would ever get to the rock without first sinking in the muck.

When his grandparents introduced him to Reverend Frazer at the door—"This is Margaret's boy come down to visit us this summer"—Peter asked the preacher, "How do you get to the rock without sinking?"

The pastor, thinking the child was talking about the swamp on Millcroft Road, said, "Just follow the yellow tufts that are in line with the giant willow."

Peter said, "Oh?" and wandered off to his grandparents' car, still puzzled about how to find the rock in his bog back home.

What Is Inside of Our Heads?

People say and hear and see what is inside of their heads, and everyone is hearing and seeing something different. "Crucified, dead, and buried." Isabel Moore grieves for her father. "Crucified, dead, and buried." The old woman cherishes the smooth-skinned, athletic Jesus. "God is a rock." Reverend Frazer is hunting in the swamp off Millcroft Road. "God is a rock." Peter Linden is in his bog back home. "God is a rock." Peter's grandparents shake their heads in agreement, and we do not know what they are seeing.

Isabel and the old woman and Peter and his grandparents are out there in the pews of your church, whether it is a cathedral with draped crosses or a country meetinghouse with the air conditioner on the blink and the old fans back in the pews. They are there taking your words and supplying the meaning from their own lives.

And Hank Afman, or someone like him, is in your church, too. I can picture Hank at the retreat I was leading. He leaned forward with his elbows on his knees because the rung of the wood chair was uncomfortable in his back. He explained, "Intimate Being. Those are my words for God. I know God is very close. Intimate. Very close. I can't think of God as a person or in terms of some image. God has got to be a being."

"God has got to be a being?" A young man with a cross made out of nails hanging on a leather thong from his neck, replied softly but skeptically. "I can't relate to a being. I need personal access to God. When I pray, I try to imagine Jesus standing there, a person who knows me. I choose 'Personal Jesus.'"

The seventeen other Presbyterian elders listened with an intensity greater than politeness. I had given all of them a copy of the following chart with instructions: "Pick one word in each column to form a prayer that represents your dominant relationship to God. If you cannot find the precise word you want in a column, supply your own. But limit it to one word, no long phrases or hyphenated constructions. The struggle to find a single word will force greater clarity within you."

Image of God		Image of Self		Image of Communication[4]	
Eternal	God	(your) believing	daughter	prays for	love
Loving	Lord	doubting	son	cries for	faith
Judging	Christ	angry	child	demands	money
Tender	Jesus	happy	disciple	wants	food
Demanding	Spirit	seeking	friend	needs	meaning
Healing	Love	trusting	priest	despairs of	comfort
Heavenly	Being	hurting	creature	wishes for	understanding
Earthly	Mother	thankful	servant	doubts	forgiveness
Unknown	Father	anxious	follower	wonders about	joy
Intimate	Savior	peaceful	rebel	thanks you for	health

After I had passed out the chart, people wiggled back into their chairs; even Hank Afman leaned against the uncomfortable rung.

Silence.

Eighteen elders sat in a circle wrestling with God instead of the building fund. They circled and erased, then furrowed their brows and circled and erased again. Some held the chart close and then far away, as though the change in distance might bring a shift of perspective inside themselves. They scribbled down alternate words, then scratched them out and wrote in new ones. And then slowly they began to look up across the circle at others, a tribe of Jacobs limping back from the Jabbok River at sunrise.

"Intimate Being." Hank spoke first.

"Personal Jesus," explained the man with the cross of two nails.

Then a woman who sat up unusually straight, but without the appearance of any stiffness in her body, said, "My relationship to God is utterly different from all of my other relationships. When I come to church I want to hear about God who is greater and better than anything else or anyone else. That's why I picked out 'Eternal.' Nothing else is eternal, only God. Eternal God."

A hard sigh came from the other side of the room. And Hank, the elder of Intimate Being, and the elder of Personal Jesus and the elder of Eternal God and all the other elders of all the other ways of calling on God who were in the room turned to listen to the bald man who was sitting beneath a church school poster of Jesus blessing the children. "I couldn't even deal with the left-hand side of the chart. So I started at the right, with what I need, with what the world needs. I am clear about that. I'm vague about God. I don't know how to call on God."

Again silence.

It was a silence even deeper than the silence during which the elders had been working on their own charts.

"I don't know how to call on God."

The words had left a giant hole in the room, as if a meteor had dropped into the middle of the circle. Some people looked at their charts to see if their image of God was still marked on the paper. Others stared into the center of the circle as if it were the center of their hearts and they were checking to make sure God was still there.

Then Hank Afman, the elder of Intimate Being, the man who

had said, "I know God is very close," spoke again, showing that God was indeed very close. "I think you have said what all of us feel sometimes in our lives and what a great many people in our congregation feel a lot of the time. It's why they come to our church: because they are vague about God and they don't know how to call on God and they want to learn."

Several elders nodded their heads yes. Then six who had not spoken shared their images of God:

"Judging Father."

"Healing Savior."

"Loving Christ."

"Unknown Love."

"Earthly Jesus."

"Tender Mother."

Eighteen elders sat in a circle telling their visions of God and no two of them agreed. When they had been ordained, they had all answered the same questions, starting with "Do you trust in Jesus Christ your Savior, acknowledge him Lord of the world and head of the church, and through him believe in one God, Father, Son, and Holy Spirit?"[5] Despite that grand affirmation of faith, they all were filled with different visions of the one Lord whom they served.

But no one said, "Shall we take a vote?" or "Will the real God please stand up?" because they sensed that the real God was already standing in the middle of the circle where their words and visions met. "There are many rooms in my Father's house," said Christ, and what those eighteen elders discovered was that they were already living in those different rooms. They shared one house of faith but they did not all live on the same floor. Some, the elder of Tender Mother and the elder of Personal Jesus and the elder of Healing Savior, felt very close to the owner. But the elders of Judging Father and Unknown Love and, above all, the elder of God the Vague felt very distant, as though they were in the cellar and the owner of the house of faith lived on the top floor.

The elders debated if it were possible for them to move from one person's room to another. Some of them said that they wanted to stay where they were.

The elder of Eternal God was put off at the prospect of Personal Jesus. "That sounds too chummy. I want God different from me, not just another friend."

But the elder of Unknown Spirit said he would like to know

Personal Jesus. He felt that "God is far, far away, like beyond the stars or the galaxies or the black holes where I can never reach." His voice sounded as though his heart were a black hole from whose gravity no personal prayer would escape. I asked him how he prayed and he said, "Oh, in very general terms. Formally. How can I feel God closer to me?"

I said to him, "Try starting a prayer with the words you want, even if their reality is not alive for you yet. If you want 'Personal Jesus,' pray to Personal Jesus. Open your prayer that way. Throw those words into the sky out beyond the stars and the black holes and maybe someday you will find someone speaking to you who has been next to you all along. I cannot promise this will happen. But it may."

Throughout the afternoon the eighteen elders walked from room to room in the house of faith that they had discovered sitting in that circle. They knocked on one another's doors, and some entered and others said no, it was too scary. One elder was silent throughout: the preacher. He said he had come to listen. And he had. He said that he talked about God every Sunday and it was his turn to hear others. Now, a preacher who listens is one whom people are eager to hear. After his long silence the eighteen elders wanted to know what the preacher had circled on the chart as his dominant image of God.

"Demanding Lord," said the preacher.

Demanding Lord?

His words crashed into the middle of the circle with an even greater impact than those of the elder who had said, "I'm vague about God. I don't know how to call on God."

Demanding Lord.

No one else all afternoon had chosen the adjective "Demanding." The preacher's dominant relationship to God was not one of seeking or comforting or healing but one of obedience, and that was what filled his sermons.

"No wonder I always feel challenged by you," said the elder of Unknown Spirit. "You are clear about what God expects while I feel God is distant, like I said, beyond the stars. How can I obey a God I don't know?"

Then seven elders spoke at once.

I lost track of the individual words and sentences because they blew around me in a mighty gust as the elders left their private rooms to look into the preacher's.

Demanding Lord.

In two words they heard again all the sermons they had ever heard from him.

Demanding Lord is a Lord who asks our obedience; a Lord who says, "I have shown you what is good: to love mercy and do justice and walk humbly with me"; a Lord who says, "Take up your cross and follow me"; a Lord who says, "I was hungry and you fed me. I was thirsty and you gave me a drink. I was naked and you clothed me." Demanding Lord! Demanding love, demanding justice, demanding compassion, demanding action, demanding heart and mind and soul and strength. Demanding Lord!

That is the vision of God whose brilliance overpowered all other visions inside the preacher. And when he told those eighteen elders sitting in the circle how often he felt lonely because he knew his vision was not the congregation's, the elders did not say to him, "Your vision is wrong" or "We want to hear no more of this." They knew that they needed his vision just as they needed one another's, because what one lacked the other had. The elders told the preacher they came to church Sunday after Sunday because they felt he was speaking the truth, a truth they needed to hear but which they had never before known so clearly until he had shared those words, "Demanding Lord." Yes, they wanted to hear about the Demanding Lord.

Sometimes it puzzled them.

Sometimes it made them angry.

Sometimes it made them squirm in their pews.

But often it made them grow. And sometimes it made them act in their families and on their jobs and in their neighborhoods. They needed the Demanding Lord but not only the Demanding Lord. Could the preacher sometimes preach about the other visions of God—about Healing Christ, Tender Mother, Earthly Jesus? Could the preacher help those for whom God was vague and distant?

The elders did not want the preacher to deny the truth and passion of his vision. They only wanted him to expand his vision, to preach the vision that was greater than his own, to declare the fullness of God, from God the Demanding Lord to God the Healing Savior.

The cook came and said the pizza would be ready in five minutes. So we all went down to the dining hall speaking softly, as if we were walking away from holy ground. When we sang the Doxology for grace, I remember looking around the room at that tribe of elders and thinking, *Praise God—Intimate Being, Personal Jesus, Tender Mother, Judging Father, Healing Savior, Loving Christ, Creator Spirit, Demanding Lord—from whom all blessings flow!*

New Rungs for Jacob's Ladder

"And [Jacob] dreamed that there was a ladder set up on the earth, and the top of it reached to heaven; and behold, the angels of God were ascending and descending on it!" (Genesis 28:12).

And Peter Linden dreamed that there was a ladder set up on the rock in the middle of the bog, and the top of it reached to the crescent moon; and behold, Peter did not know how to get to the rock without first sinking in the muck.

And the elder of Unknown Spirit dreamed that God was someplace beyond the stars and the black holes; and behold, he saw no ladder that would take him there.

Now, when Jacob awoke, he said, "'Surely the LORD is in this place; and I did not know it.'" (Genesis 28:16).

But when Peter awoke, he asked, "How do I get to the rock?"

And when the elder realized that God was painfully distant, he wanted to know, "How can I feel closer to God?"

The difference between Jacob and Peter and the elder is that one of them had a ladder to heaven and the other two did not. Who was the last one to borrow Jacob's ladder? We need it back. We need a ladder of angels to carry up prayers and to bring down visions. Does anyone around here know what happened to that ladder?

Some claim the preachers had it last and they sawed off all the rungs and tried to stake out a monopoly on God with their words. John Calvin was the head of the carpenters who did it: "Calvin, for his part, was convinced that the 'brutal stupidity' of idolatrous worship was an ineradicable symptom of man's corruption. In one form or another, it was bound always to come to the surface. 'The mind of man,' he held, 'is . . . a perpetual manufactory of idols.' One could not, therefore, guard too watchfully against this 'flagitious madness,' this 'abomination,' this 'perverse superstition.'"[6]

No doubt about it, Calvin had big ears and little eyes. Although he found communion "a mystery too sublime for me to be able to express, or even to comprehend,"[7] he still considered the visual symbols of bread and wine a concession to "our ignorance and slothfulness—and, I may add, the vanity of our minds."[8]

But Calvin is not the only one who thought the ladder of images a rickety way to heaven. There have "always been Christians, theologians and laymen both, who have doubted strongly or denied strenuously the propriety of the use of visual arts in Christian worship."[9] What else would one expect from a community of faith that believes "In the beginning was the Word . . . "? Maybe we would not keep misplacing Jacob's ladder if our sacred text read, "In the beginning was the Image. The eye knew before the mouth uttered a syllable. . . ."[10] But the word is "Word," not "Image," and oh, the difference that made to Calvin and Zwingli and the traditions and preachers that followed from them. The ear became the gate to heaven.

What, then, about those people for whom the eye is the gate to heaven? What about Peter Linden wanting to get to the rock and the woman of the smooth-skinned, athletic Jesus and the elder who looks beyond the black holes? Where is the ladder they need?

It was never completely lost. A ladder of visions showed up in the work of the greatest preachers: John Bunyan, for example—that traveling mender of pots who was imprisoned in 1660 for refusing to worship by *The Book of Common Prayer*. Bunyan's language is as rich in imagery as a medieval cathedral in statuary. In *Pilgrim's Progress* he fuses together Scripture and scenes from the English countryside to create the slough of despond, the hill of difficulty, vanity fair, the castle of doubt, giants and beasts. The gargoyles have moved from the cathedral into the cranium. No wonder *Pilgrim's Progress* became, after the Bible, the single most popular book of reformed piety. It supplied to the imagination what was denied to the eye. The icons of glass and stone had been carried away only for their ghosts to reappear through Bunyan's words. And not just through Bunyan but also through every preacher who discovered that "thought is pictorial"[11] and that

> Words strain,
> Crack and sometimes break, under the burden,
> Under the tension, slip, slide, perish,
> Decay with imprecision, will not stay in place,
> Will not stay still. . . .[12]

It takes stories and images to keep those slippery, sliding words in place. That is why we preachers are always trying to rebuild Jacob's ladder with sermon illustrations. The ineptitude of our approach is that we often end up with unevenly spaced rungs. For ten minutes we talk about "the meaning and building of Christian community." Then for one minute we illustrate with a scene we saw last week on the playground: a second grader in a plaid shirt shared some potato chips with a classmate. Next we are back to our discourse on the principles of community and the implications of empathetic living. Finally we offer a closing illustration from our own lives: a Finn who also spoke English helped us order a ham sandwich in a remote town on the Arctic Circle.

Ask the congregation at the door what they remember out of the sermon.

The potato chips and the ham sandwich.

Of course!

But the two stories were separated by such large gaps of generalized reflection that people could not reach from one to the other. The stories were anecdotes rather than revelations.

We preachers need to build our sermons so that our listeners can step securely from image to image, story to story and thus climb up into the truth of their lives.

"And behold, the angels of God were ascending and descending" on Jacob's ladder. Note this: the angels go up before they come down. Don't start in heaven. Don't start with the sweeping generality "This morning I would like to share some reflection with you on the complex task of building Christian community." Send an angel up before you send one down. Start on earth. Start with the particular, with what we see and hear and touch.[13]

"I once walked into a restaurant in Rovaniemi, Finland, only to discover that no one spoke a word of English. With the waiter at my side, I put my left palm up on the table and pretended to spread it with butter. Then I placed my right hand on top of my left and lifted them both to my mouth. The waiter walked away laughing. I was sure he understood, but twenty minutes later I still had no food.

"Then a man came in who spoke thick but perfect English. He ordered a ham sandwich for me and the waiter who had been baffled by my pantomine brought it in a minute. . . ."

The story is no longer an "illustration" of some general principle. Rather, it is the first rung upward toward the experience and exploration of our theme. In this short human scene the great issues of building community are already before us:

strangers who cannot communicate; the importance of someone who can translate needs to others so that they can respond; hunger and feeding. The sermon is in the scene as a plant is in the seed, waiting to unfurl its compressed genetic springs into root, stem, leaf, flower, fruit. The congregation will hear the Word through what they see blossoming in the scene.

Unless a Child

> We are climbing Jacob's ladder,
> We are climbing Jacob's ladder,
> We are climbing Jacob's ladder,
> Soldiers of the cross.

Children's voices spook across a lake from a campfire to the accompaniment of bullfrogs and crickets. The children have the ladder of visions for which we have been looking. They can teach us preachers how to climb it.

—Don't be ridiculous. It's just a song and they're just kids. A sentimental scene—

You are right—just a song and just kids, some of them with their arms around each other's shoulders, feeling the earliest nudgings of romance and glad that the night around them is black and that only their faces show in the campfire. And you are right about the scene's being sentimental. But have you ever preached on the text ". . . unless you turn and become like children, you will never enter the kingdom of heaven" (Matthew 18:3)? I once heard a three-point sermon on becoming a child. Have you ever known a child who came up to you and said, "Now, there are three points I would like to make about your buying me an ice-cream cone"? The sermon did not help me become like a child because the preacher had not become like a child.

> We are climbing Jacob's ladder,
> We are climbing Jacob's ladder,
> We are climbing Jacob's ladder,
> Soldiers of the cross.

The lake between the children's song and us is dark and deep with fearful water. Yet there is another voice, also a child's, though closer to us than the distant shore. It is the child within us, buried by the deposits of adulthood but calling to us from forgotten depths and telling us to cross the lake silent as a lily pad and sneak into the children's circle.

Go.

Now.

Go as a child, not an adult.

Watch the fire.

Build castles out of flame.

Imagine yourself falling in love with someone beautiful, kind, and good. The person next to you with fingers sticky from melted marshmallow will do.

> Look at the stars! look, look up at the skies!
> O look at all the fire-folk sitting in the air! [14]

Join the singing.

> We are climbing Jacob's ladder,
> We are climbing Jacob's ladder,
> We are climbing Jacob's ladder,
> Soldiers of the cross.

Yes. Yes! YOU are climbing Jacob's ladder. You are climbing it with the children. You are climbing it with the slaves who first sang that song and who called upon God through "concrete imagery rather than abstract thought." [15] And in the pulpit you will be able to climb that ladder with your people, not because you have mastered the latest homiletical technique but because you have reengaged the visionary capacities of the child within you.

"The physicist J. Robert Oppenheimer once said, 'There are children playing in the streets who could solve some of my top problems in physics, because they have modes of sensory perception that I lost long ago.'" [16] And there are children wiggling in the pews who could solve some of the preacher's top problems in communication because of their modes of sensory perception.

"How do I get to the rock without first sinking in the muck?" Peter Linden's question reveals the way a child experiences and interprets the world through his or her senses. I could analyze Peter's language like the three-point sermon on childhood that I heard. Our biblical text, however, reads ". . . unless you . . . *become* like children"—become, not talk about, not break into concepts, not philosophize on, but *become*. So let us become like children by entering Peter's world and experiencing it through his sensory modes of perception.

The Top of Things

When Peter walked into the room, Aunt Almeda propped

herself up in bed and her quilt slipped to the floor. She was wearing a checked wool shirt over her nightgown, even though the August sun had started to bake the tin-roofed cabin. The bed seemed to be growing out of the floor, as though its legs were connected to roots that spread beneath the litter of newspapers and clothes and unwashed soup bowls and coffee cups. Next to the bed was a sawed-off oil barrel fitted with a wooden seat from an outhouse.

"It's a matter of pride with your Aunt Almeda," Peter's grandfather had told him on the way over, "that she still goes to the bathroom and cooks by herself. The visiting nurse said she shouldn't get out of bed because the arthritis is so bad in her ankles and knees that she's wearing away her joints. But Almeda said she'd order her body to hell before some nurse could tell her what she could and couldn't do. I made her a little johnny out of an old oil barrel and bought a hot plate down at the Corners. Every few days I go by to empty the barrel and to take her dishes into the kitchen and clean them. She's really looking forward to seeing you."

Almeda kicked the sheets down to the floor and swung her legs over the bed and waved Peter toward her.

"So you're Margaret's boy. Come here and let me see you closer."

Peter stepped toward the old woman and tried not to hold his nose.

The walls around Almeda's bed were papered with photographs from *Life* and *Look,* yellowed with age. By focusing on them, Peter found he could take his mind off his nose, at least a little.

"What are you looking at, Son?"

"The pictures on the wall."

"You like those? I put them all up myself. Some of them I tore out just because they're pretty. But others, they remind me of something I once seen or dreamed. You recognize any?"

"I've been here," said Peter, pointing to a photograph of the Empire State Building. He remembered how his folks had taken him there and how disappointed they were that they could only see as far as Hoboken because of the haze that day.

"I was always going to go to New York City, Peter, and go up to the top of things, to the top of the Statue of Liberty and to the top of the Empire State Building. Years ago I sent for a map from there and I studied that map for weeks and pretended

I was walking around seeing all the sights. I figured I'd arrive at Grand Central Station and step around the corner a few blocks to Sachs Fifth Avenue and buy me a real lady's dress like those ones in this picture," Almeda said, pointing to an ad of some high society women in long evening gowns. "Then I'd hire a taxi and say, 'Central Park East' and check into the Park Lane Hotel. It would be terribly expensive, but I'd figured I could afford it for just one night if when I took the train I went in the sitting car instead of the Pullman and if I didn't buy no sandwiches from the porter but took my own food. Then I'd live like the richest lady in the world for one day and one night in New York City, going to the top of things and to fancy shops and to the circus in Madison Square Garden. I'd saved up over half the cost in seven years from my egg money. Then Alex went and robbed that store up in Lexington, and your granddad here and I had to scrape together every cent we had to hire some lawyer. That wiped out my egg money and I never took no trip. Right, Bud?" Almeda said to Peter's grandfather.

"Yeah, Sis, I don't suppose we can ever forget it: our family name dragged in the papers and all the gossip. But at least Alex saw the light and accepted Jesus before he died."

"Yes, at least there's that. I suppose that him and Mom is in heaven now, walking around on the top of things and not fighting about his drinking anymore."

Almeda was silent for a moment, then shifted her position on the bed and said to Peter, "Son, how's your mom?"

"Oh, she's fine, Aunt Almeda. She remembers you a lot. She's told me about the swimming hole out back."

"She has? That hole isn't there anymore now, you know. I mean, there is a hole there but there hasn't been any water in it for nearly fifteen years. When they started the new mine up the hill, they turned the stream back down the other side and the hole dried up. Although the last few years some brush and scrub trees started growing there." Peter looked so let down that Almeda wondered if he had planned to take a swim that morning.

"You can go out back and see for yourself. There isn't no water there."

"I believe you, Aunt Almeda. I don't think I want to see it anyway. I was just interested because Mom has often mentioned it, especially whenever she's read the pool of Bethesda story with me."

"Oh, Peter, is Margaret reading the Bible with you?"

"Every morning, Aunt Almeda."

"And you ought to hear him read the Bible by himself, Sis," said Peter's grandfather. "This morning Lottie and I had him read us about the healing of the ten lepers and he did just fine. He says all of them words real clear, like he knows the story. I told him maybe someday he'd be a preacher."

"A preacher!" exclaimed Almeda. "Oh, wouldn't that be fine. It might make up for Alex and all the harm he did this family."

"Now, Sis, remember what you said about Alex and Mom up in heaven. The Lord forgave Alex and we've forgiven him, too."

Almeda's eyes shifted to the Empire State Building and then back to Peter. "Do you pray, too, Son?"

"Yes. Every morning after we read the Bible, we pray."

"Well then, come right close now and say a prayer with me." Almeda reached her arm out and pointed to the barrel. "You can sit right here on the edge, Peter, so I can hold your hand."

Peter sat down on the johnny and reached his right hand to Almeda's. He felt her wrinkled palms and knobby knuckles.

"Now, you pray for me, Peter. You pray for your old Aunt Almeda."

Peter sat on the barrel and wondered if now it were safe to hold his nose with his free hand since his aunt and grandfather both had their eyes shut. He wished his mother were there. She always knew what to say to Jesus. He recalled his mother's favorite first sentence: "Jesus, thank you for the morning." Peter spoke the words aloud.

Aunt Almeda whispered, "Thank you, Jesus."

The word "morning" made Peter think of the day. So he prayed again, "Jesus, thank you for the day."

"Thank you, Jesus," whispered his aunt again.

Now Peter was stumped. He opened his eyes. Aunt Almeda and his grandfather still had theirs shut. He knew they were expecting more. Then Peter saw the pictures.

"Jesus, thank you for the pictures."

"Thank you," whispered Aunt Almeda.

"Jesus, thank you for the Empire State Building."

"Thank you," whispered Aunt Almeda again.

Her "thank yous" gave Peter courage, and she seemed to like thanking Jesus for the pictures; so Peter started picking out pictures from the wall and thanking Jesus for them. And after every picture his aunt whispered, "Thank you."

"Jesus, thank you for the Statue of Liberty."

"Thank you."

"Jesus, thank you for the women in the long black dresses."

"Thank you."

"Jesus, thank you for the subway."

"Thank you."

"Jesus, thank you for the elephant."

"Thank you."

Peter worried that he would have to thank Jesus for every single picture. There were dozens of them. Then he looked at his aunt. "Jesus, thank you for Aunt Almeda."

"Thank you."

"Jesus, thank you for her hands."

"Thank you."

Almeda tried to squeeze Peter's hand, but her joints were so swollen that she could not really close on it. Peter looked at her hand when he felt it moving and thought it must hurt a lot, and he remembered his mother praying with him when he was sick.

"Jesus, heal Aunt Almeda."

"Heal me, Jesus," she whispered.

"Jesus, help Aunt Almeda."

"Help me, Jesus. Help me, Jesus! Help me, Jesus!!"

His aunt's voice was rising above a whisper and it scared Peter. He did not know what she would expect him to do or say next. Peter panicked. "Thank you, Jesus, and amen." Peter said the words quickly and with finality.

"Amen," whispered Aunt Almeda, much to Peter's relief.

Peter lifted away his hand. His aunt opened her eyes and his grandfather walked up to the bed and put his hand on Peter's shoulder. All three were silent for a moment.

"Well, I guess we gotta be going, Sis. I promised to drive Peter up to Hinman's Hollow after we came by here."

"Yes, I guess you gotta be going. It's been a nice visit. Peter, you're a fine boy. You tell your mother that I'm proud of her, that she's got a son like you."

"Good-bye, Aunt Almeda."

"Good-bye, Peter. I hope you like Hinman's Hollow. Along with my swimming hole it was always your mother's favorite place to visit when she was a child."

The "modes of sensory perception" that J. Robert Oppenheimer and the preachers lost are alive and well in Peter Linden.

Peter looks at the cabin wall strewn with photographs and sees a universe. Peter feels Almeda's knobby hand and knows it hurts. Peter smells the barrel and calls to Jesus while sitting on its edge. His prayer, like Jacob's ladder, sends angels up to heaven, then calls the Savior down.

I have used Peter's story as a sermon in several churches. I might have preached the message in an entirely different manner. I could have built what I wanted to say into a classic three-point sermon, enumerated and ordered according to reason:

Point 1: To minister to people requires that we enter their world and observe and understand what is important to them.

Point 2: Entering their world requires being alive to the presence of God through our senses, as children are alive to what they see, smell, and feel.

Point 3: We can lift up the person's world (point 1) and respond to God's presence (point 2) in prayer.

Instead I wrote, "When Peter walked into the room, Aunt Almeda propped herself up in bed and her quilt slipped to the floor. . . ."

I have preached the sermon at three different churches: a sophisticated suburban church, a church in a rural town, and an ecumenical gathering. In every case I used James 5:13-18 as a text and highlighted the words "pray for one another, that you may be healed," quoting them before and after the story. In each setting the response has been more than "nice sermon" or "I enjoyed your message." People came out and told me stories of prayers they had offered with others or stories about pictures that meant a great deal to them or stories about old people they had meant to visit and never did but now would or stories about arthritis or stories about their own prayer life and how they had never realized they could pray with their eyes open. I gave the sermon being. The listeners supplied the meaning.

> We are climbing Jacob's ladder,
> We are climbing Jacob's ladder,
> We are climbing Jacob's ladder,
> Soldiers of the cross.

We are climbing it rung by rung, stepping from the Empire State Building to the women in black dresses to the elephant to Almeda's knobby hands to Jesus who heals us. We are climbing Jacob's ladder from vision to vision, story to story. We are climbing it by using the modes of sensory perception that lead us into the heart of reality.

> Every step goes higher, higher,
> Every step goes higher, higher,
> Every step goes higher, higher,
> Soldiers of the cross.

Salted Eggs and a Muddy River Bank

Morning. The ladder and the song have vanished. We awake from the children's enchanted night to see the sun shining on a blemished world.

Make the coffee.

Put on the eggs.

Push down the toast.

We have to be to the office by 8 A.M.

"Then Jacob awoke from his sleep and said, 'Surely the LORD is in this place; and I did not know it'" (Genesis 28:16). His midnight dream reveals to Jacob the presence of God in the wide-awake world. And the preacher's ladder of visions does the same for the congregation: it connects heaven and earth so that members of the congregation become aware of the Holy One in their midst. The images and stories are more than sermon illustrations. They train the congregation's eye to see into the depths of daily life. "Surely the LORD is in this place; and I did not know it." Jacob's words become the congregation's words.

The toast is up. The coffee's done. "I salt my breakfast eggs. All day long I feel created."[17] The preacher at the church I was visiting yesterday quoted that and I have been tasting it in my memory ever since. There was a lot in that sermon: the Genesis story about our being made from dust and a reference to the creed—"Maker of heaven and earth"—and a plea about the environment and this line: "I salt my breakfast eggs. All day long I feel created." And now today I am salting my eggs, and I feel created! I feel my bones hammered out of the same calcium that is in the rocks and hinged together with elastic molecules like those in the birch that bends in the wind. Yesterday's sermon brings me to Monday's breakfast table as astounded as Jacob: "Surely the LORD is in this place; and I did not know it." I sit at this maple kitchen table with the green calendar hanging next to the wall phone and note the dates I have circled and the appointments I have to keep, my life plotted out by number, like one of those childhood books in which you draw from dot to dot, only now it is from date to date and hour to hour. I sit here and feel the heft of life's simplest tasks: trying to get the frozen orange juice out of the container and measuring the coffee before I have had any to drink and getting up to bring the salt over for the eggs. The salt! I can hear the preacher: "'I salt my breakfast eggs. All day long I feel created.'" I am created. God created me. I live. It's Monday morning, but I live. I live because it's a gift. I live because God loves me. O God, thank you.

The materiality of the preacher's sermon lives on in the materiality of the listener's world. The congregation can hear the Spirit still speaking after the preacher sits down, because the preacher has proclaimed the Spirit through the world the listeners know, through the world of salt and eggs, through the world of water and stone, blood and muscle that the Bible describes: "The Old and New Testaments are unremittingly physical in their articulation, like most other sane human narrations—action follows and is generally caused by sensory perception of some previous action. Failure to convey that reality is failure to tell the story, failure to confront and recreate (in a language like English, equally capable of the reality) the embarrassing and demanding corporeality of the original."[18] About the only place where one does not find that corporeality is in modern versions of Scripture! "It is a failure endemic to most contemporary translations"[19] that they water down the plain, anthropomorphic language that gives the Bible its power of personal engagement. "What the abstractionists are saying is plain—'The original, of course, employed its resources of limited vocabulary and primitive imagery to the limit, but what we must tell you is what they *meant* to say.'"[20]

Unfortunately, preachers often follow the lead of the translators and become "abstractionists" themselves: "I want to speak to you this morning about the meaning and building of Christian community." No! Do not give your people the meaning of community. Give them the embarrassing and demanding corporeality of community, the way the Gospel writers do when they picture members of a crowd passing bread and fish to one another or the disciples squabbling about who is going to get a seat of honor in the kingdom or Jesus washing and wiping their feet. And if the pious decoupage we have layered over the

Bible is still hiding the embarrassing and demanding corporeality of the text, then strip it away with one small detail that gives the weight of daily life to heaven's revelation:

> Jesus stepped in the mud
> of the river Jordan
> in front of a large crowd
> and his cousin John.
> He wanted to be baptized,
> he said.[21]

"Slurp, whack, slurp, whack." Peter Linden listens to the preacher and imagines Jesus walking through his bog. The old lady waiting for the smooth-skinned, athletic Savior moves her eyes suddenly to the pulpit, listening to see how the preacher is going to clean Jesus up. The elder of God the Vague is intrigued by a Jesus dressed in mud instead of clouds of glory. Even Isabel Moore, grieving for her father, is hooked by the single word "mud." It reminds her of the grave. For these few opening seconds the preacher has them all.

> John,
> that cousin,
> was horrified
> when Jesus
> bent before him
> in the mud,
>   and to understand the horror of John
>   we must know something more about that mud.[22]

The preacher focuses on the single detail that is pulling Peter Linden, the old lady, the elder, and Isabel Moore into the sermon. The preacher tells them more about the mud—the mud of Noah's flood, the mud of the Red Sea, the mud of human evil, and then, at last, the glory:

> But he, Jesus,
> he went down,
> and when he came up,
> the mud still streaming from his ears,
> over his eyes
> and his nose
> into his mouth,
>   HEAVEN OPENED,
>   and a voice was heard,
>   and a Spirit,
>   a new Spirit in people,
>   a new life

and a new heart
were announced,
glory, glory, alleluia.[23]

Glory, glory, alleluia and slurp, whack, slurp, whack, thinks Peter,
playing in his bog with Jesus. "Glory, glory, alleluia," feels the
old lady who today leaves church knowing that her smooth-
skinned, athletic Savior is also with her when she visits the
nursing home to see her sister. "Glory, glory, alleluia." The
elder of God the Vague is not yet filled with such praise, and
Isabel Moore is still grieving, but both of them leave church with
a hope that is nudging its way into their hearts. For the preacher
said at the end that Jesus was not going to forget the mud:

> because once he got
> the Spirit,
> that Spirit drove him
> into the desert,
> and then again
> out of the desert,
>   to do his work
>   in this world,
>   to struggle with evil in us,
>   in the world,
>   in this world,
>   in order to overcome it.[24]

The gospel thunders through details that connect it to the life
we know. "I salt my breakfast eggs. All day long I feel created."
I scrape mud off my boots when I come in from the garden and
I hear the preacher once again: "Jesus stepped in the mud of
the river Jordan." Salt and mud are rungs on Jacob's ladder close
to earth, single syllable words, elements of life as natural as a
baby screaming his head off during his dedication:

Zacharias said, firmly and quietly:
"His name is John."
There was general astonishment and some went down on their
knees. Zacharias, as if to make up for the long enforced dumbness,
became voluble and prophetic. His son howled, and the father
shouted him down. Zacharias was most articulate and his sentences
were beautifully woven, and one may not doubt that what he now
said he had rehearsed long though in silence. He said:
"Blessed be the Lord, the God of Israel. For he has visited us
and wrought redemption for his people. He has raised for us a
horn of salvation in the house of his servant David." John was so
loud that it was as if he were blowing a horn of a different kind.
His mother rocked and hushed him, but he only bellowed the
louder. "And what he spoke through the mouths of the holy

prophets shall be fulfilled—salvation from our enemies, and from
the hand of all that hate us—mercy to his people, who shall serve
him without fear, in holiness and righteousness before him all our
days."

Zacharias seemed to many to be going on too long, but the only
voice of protest was the child's, and Zacharias had almost to bellow
himself to say:

"And you, my child, whose voice is already great and shall be
greater still in the Lord's service—" Many smiled at this, but not
Zacharias. "—You shall be called the Prophet of the Most High,
for you shall go before the face of the Lord to make ready his path,
to give knowledge of salvation to his people, in the remission of
their sins, because of the tender mercy of our God."

His final words on this holy and indeed miraculous occasion are
said by some to have been sung by him in a fine priestly voice,
and indeed there is a quality of song about them:

"Whereby the dayspring from on high shall visit us, to shine
upon them that sit in darkness and the shadow of death, to guide
our feet into the way of peace." He hung his head, eyes closed,
and prayed silently. The infant John was given the breast.[25]

Baby John the Baptist cries during the sacred moment in the
temple, and all of the parents of all of the children who have
ever cried in church know that the Benedictus that Zacharias
bellows above his son's protesting voice is meant for them. The
tears of the child are rungs on Jacob's ladder close to earth that
lead us on toward heaven. "Blessed be the Lord, the God of
Israel," who gave us this child crying in our arms. Blessed be
the Lord, who has visited and redeemed screaming children,
embarrassed parents, fumbling clergy, and grinning congregations. Blessed be the Lord. Amen and amen.

Hefty Angels

If Jacob's ladder reaches to heaven, salt, mud, and tears remind us that it also dents the earth. Hefty angels climb up and
down that ladder. The vision that God delivers is about this
world and this life: "Surely the LORD is *in this place;* and I did
not know it." In this place where Jacob wakes up with a kink
in his neck from using a rock for a pillow, in this place where
our congregations trace their weeks on the kitchen calendar, in
this place has God been present and they did not know it. But
now they know it. They know it from the sermon that etched
pictures in the air of the sanctuary, and they know it from the
face, the gestures, the body, the presence of the preacher, as I
discovered from a parishioner who said: "A black robe can be
very severe, you know." She was sitting in my office on Monday

morning. "After last week"—the woman's husband had lost his job and her baby had been hospitalized—"I came into church yesterday and looked at you up there in that robe and thought, *God is in a black robe like a judge, ready to judge me.* And I got angry at God. I could see God standing in heaven saying, 'Give her husband a pink slip and make her baby sick.' Then you came down out of the pulpit and sat next to me and put your arm up behind me in the pew while we listened to the solo. And the reason I cried was not because of anything particular in the sermon or the prayers, but because when you put your arm around me, I thought, *God loves me. God's not angry with me* and I was so glad, I couldn't help crying."

Nor could the woman help crying that morning in my office as she explained her tears from the day before. Nor have I been able to get the story out of my mind. On Saturday night, when I am still struggling with the words for tomorrow, I hear the woman's voice and see her tears. "When you put your arm around me at the back of the pew, I thought, *God loves me.*" How many words about God's love have I thrown into the air only to discover they evaporated before they landed in anyone's heart? Then one Sunday I sit with a sad parishioner in the pew and the vault of heaven swings open and grace swoops down into her bruised soul. "God loves me. God's not angry with me," the woman said. A preacher cannot plan something like that. It's grace. It's redemption. It's the wind blowing where it will. You can't ask the ushers to turn it on with a switch in the narthex, and you cannot put it in the manuscript. "And the reason I cried was not because of anything particular in the sermon or the prayers." If angels are going to come down Jacob's ladder from heaven, as well as go up from earth, it will have to be through more than words alone. I think of preachers I have heard whose text was "God is love" but whose voices shredded the air with anger or who spoke on the "hope of the gospel" with fear in their eyes and a body bowed beneath a hidden, heavy weight. What image of God is controlling the timbre of our voice and the motions of our body? When our people look at us, what do they see—a face disfigured with public piety (Matthew 6:16) or a face like Esau's, welcoming home Jacob who burst out in gratitude, ". . . truly to see your face is like seeing the face of God, with such favor have you received me" (Genesis 33:10)? That must have been no plastic grin that Esau flashed at his brother, the shyster who had always been Mom's favorite and who had tricked Esau out of his father's blessing. People are not good at faking forgiveness. Oh, they can hand out a few words of greeting like ice cubes: "Hello, Jacob. It has been a long time. We've been waiting for you." But a face filled with favor, a face with dancing eyes and a smile leaping up from the heart, a face like God's can come only from God.

What was true for Esau is true for us preachers. We can change our words. We can give our people visions and voices. We can make our language bristle with life. But the vision that matters most is the vision that runs in the blood. That is why we must not escape to ordering ink for the mimeograph machine when what we need is time to be refilled ourselves with the surge of God's love. If God is vague for the preacher, no amount of eloquence will stir the congregation to belief. If God is an Ever Angry Judge for the preacher, words of grace stacked from the floor to the rafters of the sanctuary will not squeeze the acid out of the air. But if the preacher knows God as a Tender Mother or a Heavenly Father, then light will shine irrepressible in the eyes, and the voice will ring with the confidence of faith. The preacher, no matter how lean and lanky, will appear in the pulpit as the heftiest angel of all, a human being who has a personal message from God, a human being who has climbed up and down Jacob's ladder getting ready for Sunday morning. The congregation may not use Jacob's exact words, but in their own way they will sense "to see your face is like seeing the face of God, with such favor have you received me." It won't be because you are handsome, beautiful, great, or good, but because you yourself have been received with favor by God. Isabel Moore, her eyes still lined with grief, will look at you and flash a little bit of her old smile. The lady of the smooth-skinned, athletic Jesus will say at the door, "You helped me today." Peter Linden will skip out grinning. The elder of God the Vague will shake hands with a stronger grip. And as you watch them walk from the church, you will sense that a certain slant of light has penetrated their daily world and that, like Jacob at Bethel, they realize "Surely the LORD is in this place; and I did not know it."

supplied family stores in suburban New Jersey and a few in the city. I supervised the processing while Aud kept the books. We made a good living, good enough that in 1952 we bought fifteen acres near Shandaken, New York, and hired a contractor to build us a cabin: two small bedrooms, a cramped bath, and a combination living-dining-kitchen area. This was before the craze for cedar cabins and the natural look. It was a one-story frame structure with a screened-in porch off the back and a single-paned picture window in the front. The driveway came up to the porch and the only door into the place was on that back wall. It may sound like a strange way to build a cabin, but Aud had designed it that way for a reason. She wanted to watch the wild deer that came almost every day to a small pond in front of the cabin. That was why we had bought the land in the first place, because the farmer who had sold it promised we would see plenty of deer there."

The elder of Unknown Spirit moves his hand to his wife's. They have just bought some land in the country. "To be closer to nature" he tells his friends; although if you could look into his heart, you would see he is hoping God will come to him there.

The detail of the deer had been suggested to the preacher's mind by the psalm for the day: "As a hart longs/for flowing streams,/so longs my soul/for thee, O God" (Psalm 42:1).

"I met Aud skiing, a sport I had taken up because I wanted one my parents had never tried. I was a novice when I "scraggled" up to Aud on my skis. I had just watched her glide down the hill with grace, and my first words to her were 'How did you do that?' I do not recall hers because I was so impressed with her beauty. She had a broad, pleasant face with the smile of someone who enjoys a party so long as she is not the center of attention."

Andrea Winston's husband repeats in his head what he tells every visitor who is puzzled by the bust of his wife: *She's a beauty and she doesn't see it.* And while the preacher moves over his manuscript page, Andrea's eyes shift for an instant to her husband, and the smile missing from her statue passes over her lips.

"Both my parents were gym teachers in Passaic. Dad had played first-string quarterback for Springfield College and my mother was a gymnastics star when she was at Ithaca. But I was born a goose, not a swan. I can recall as a very little boy my father getting angry with me because when he threw a football to me I would carry it to the driveway and try to spin it like a top."

The elder of Tender Mother almost calls out from the pew to let the child spin the ball. And the elder of Judging Father constricts the muscles beneath his eyes to dam back the tears.

"During high school my father and mother insisted that if I were not playing sports I could at least find myself a job. I did. I became a butcher's assistant at Kunstler's Pork and Sausage.

"When I returned from the war, I bought the store from Jacob Kunstler and then met Aud skiing. I brought her to meet my parents in late April of that year. They had a badminton net set up in the back yard, and my mother offered to play Aud. After watching for five minutes, my father said, 'Well, I'll be; she's got your mother's grace. What does she see in you?' I ignored the dig because the smile on my father's face told me that he approved of Aud. After she and I were married, I felt more welcome in my parents' home than I ever had as a child."

The preacher scans the congregation. They have never listened so intensely.

"Something else happened, too. For the first time in my life I mastered a sport. Under Aud's instruction I became an expert skier, though not as fine as she. I hired a photographer to take a movie of me. When my father saw me swinging down the slopes on the screen, he said: 'That's you, Son?! You look as good as Duke Frampton picking his way through the secondary.' Duke Frampton was the best high school halfback my father had ever coached.

"When the movie shut off, I went up to Aud and whispered, 'Thank you. I love you so much.' Then I went into the bathroom and cried."

The elder of Unknown Spirit squeezes his wife's hand. If God seems beyond the stars and the black holes where he can never reach, at least at this moment in his pew the elder is appreciating how God's love may be coming to him through his wife.

"When I turned sixty, we decided to sell our meat business and retire to the cabin. Although it was mostly a summer place, we had winterized it for ski weekends. Every time we stayed there while the children were growing up, we dreamed of someday living in those mountains where Aud and I had met.

"That first and only autumn in the cabin we watched the leaves blaze, fade, and fall. Then in early November we yearned with the naked woods for the snow. We were not walking anywhere in the forest because we could hear the guns. Our land was posted and we stayed close to the cabin. Aud would not drive to town during the day for fear she would see a deer on top of some hunter's car. How she loved those animals. That is why we built the cabin, so she could watch them. When a hunter wandered onto our property one morning, Aud went out in her housecoat and yelled at him to leave.

"It was exactly a week later—I remember because Aud noted it at breakfast—that we heard some shots from behind the cabin, maybe a quarter of a mile away. She handed me an old cowbell we kept on the mantle and said, 'Go out ringing this and tell them the land is posted.' I put on my red jacket and went out the back door. I stopped on the porch a minute and called for Aud to hand me my hat and gloves. The temperature must have been in the thirties. As I walked down the steps of the porch, I looked up and saw a great buck coming frantically down our driveway. The deer ran around front and I saw two hunters about fifty yards behind the cabin. 'You take that side of the house,' called one to the other. I started shouting, 'The land is posted. The land is posted.' But they were intent on that deer. I ran around the cabin before they did. The buck was standing like a statue in the front yard. I could see Aud at the picture window, her face tense for the animal.

"Both hunters came around the sides of the cabin at the same time. The buck thought he was cornered and lept through the window before the hunters could fire a shot. The heavy plate glass tore open his neck, and he crashed into Aud. I could see him bucking and kicking. Then he collapsed.

"I ran into the cabin.

"Aud was dead, her head kicked in by the crazed deer. The animal took a few more breaths. Then silence.

"The next night after the police had gone and some neighbors had cleaned the place, I returned. The smell reminded me of the butcher shop. I brought the skis in from the porch and piled them in the middle of the living room. Then I took the Bernzomatic torch with which we used to apply our base wax and set the skis on fire.

"I walked out the door and went to the front lawn. A deer was at the pond. I do not know whether it was a buck or a doe. It ran away, and I walked back around the cabin and down the driveway crying, my body stiff and awkward."

The preacher moves the manuscript aside and puts the Bible back on the pulpit stand, opened to the lesson, a few verses underlined.

"Hear again from the word of God," says the preacher.

An unarticulated prayer springs from the congregation: "O God, yes, what word do you have for our slaughtered dreams and our broken lives?"

"Love bears all things, believes all things, hopes all things, endures all things" (1 Corinthians 13:7).

These words, have we heard them before? Yes, many times, but never like this. After that story they are like a familiar picture with a new frame. We see colors and lines that we missed before. They are like a shout in Isabel Moore's soul that rouses new strength in her body; and though she weeps today, she weeps with hope as well as grief.

"Love never ends . . ." (1 Corinthians 13:8).

The elder of Unknown Spirit spontaneously prays, "O Dear God of Love, may it be true," and God flashes for an instant from beyond the black holes of space into the black hole of the man's heart.

"For now we see in a mirror dimly, but then face to face . . ." (1 Corinthians 13:12).

Andrea Winston's husband looks at his wife whose eyes are shining because she has caught a glimpse of what she means to him.

"So faith, hope, love abide, these three; but the greatest of these is love" (1 Corinthians 13:13).

Silence again.

Like starving people finally receiving food, the congregation needs time for each word so that it is not eaten too quickly to be absorbed. Then the preacher prays the truth home:

"O Tender and Eternal God, we need your love.
We need your love that bears all things,
                    believes all things,
                    hopes all things,
                    endures all things.
We need your love.
We need your love to come through our friends,
                    through our children,
                    through our neighbors,
                    through our husbands and wives.

And when they are taken from us, we need your love that never ends.

We need your love to carry on and to share with others so
that we do not become noisy gongs or clanging cymbals.
We need your love.
For Christ's sake. Amen."

Was It a Sermon?

No.
The story was not in itself a sermon. It was a human love
story. But the way the preacher put the story together with the
reading of the Bible lesson and the prayer was a sermon, a three-
part—not three-point—sermon. Part one was opening the congregation's heart. That was the function of the story, to get
people ready to receive God's Word. It was deliberately not
religious. Most people do not live in a religious world. They live
in the world of broken human relationships, of unfair parents
who demand what children cannot give, and of tragic deaths
that cut off those to whom they look for their salvation. Of
course, God's love is addressed directly to this world, but sermons often do not make that clear because they pull this world
in as a source of illustration rather than exploring it as the locus
of struggle and meaning. It is here, in this nonreligious world,
that our listeners wrestle with the Lord as doggedly as Jacob
did. Though they may not use the same language as the ancient
tale from Genesis, still they tighten every muscle and stretch
every tendon and call up every reserve of energy to take on the
great issues of life and death. Through their questions, their
decisions, their arguments, and their suffering they fight—sometimes with and sometimes against—the One who rules all of
creation.

Part two of the sermon was the rereading of the selected
verses from the Bible. These words have been heard so often
that the preacher's task is to help people hear them as though
for the first time. The story is meant to create a receptivity for
the sacred words. By drawing on the depths of the human soul
through Aud's death, the preacher is engaging the congregation's thirst and hunger for a greater reality.

Part three is the carefully planned prayer in which the preacher
is drawing together the pain awakened by the story and the
hope and healing offered by the Scripture. This is where the
message of God's love becomes incarnate: "We need your love
to come through our friends, through our children, through our
neighbors, through our husbands and wives."

The proportion of gospel to world in the total sermon—story, Scripture, prayer—is small if you are counting words that mention God or Christ or the Bible. But it is large if you look at the impact on Isabel Moore, the elder of Unknown Spirit, Andrea Winston and her husband. The story has aroused in them a desire for God's love. The preacher now must entrust the remaining work of redemption to the restlessness of that desire and to God, who can alone satisfy it.

"Is this finished?" asked a visitor to the studio of Henry Moore, the famous sculptor. Moore answered: "None of my work is finished until it is seen and responded to."[10]

It is the same with sermons, especially the kind of three-part story sermon we are examining here. The sermon is not over when the preacher steps out of the pulpit. Isabel Moore will complete the sermon when she breaks out of her stifling grief to share love with others. Andrea Winston will finish the preacher's message when she claims the beauty that is hers. The elder of Unknown Spirit will say his own amen when he realizes how God's love is moving toward him through his wife. The conclusion of the sermon lies beyond worship in the continuing life of the congregation and its witness in the world.

We preachers do not have the last word. Our listeners do. They must spell out with their lives the gospel we present with our voices. We preachers are like those people who carried their paralyzed friend to Jesus. Unless they carried the man to Him, he would never have walked on his own. But the healing itself was not in their hands. It came from Christ. The story of Aud and her death carries members of the congregation to Christ by drawing out their own paralyzing doubts and fears and tragedies. By offering such a story in worship, the preacher is saying that it is all right to bring your deepest hurts to Christ. You do not have to be religious to come to Christ, just human. Bring your own broken self-image to Christ and Christ will restore it. Aud's husband walks back down the driveway crying, his body stiff and awkward, and his halting steps remind us of our stiffness and our awkwardness. Through that widower's grief we discover our own need for grace of body, grace of soul, and we hunger for the love that never ends.

The Savior with the Puffy Eyelids

From the circle of eighteen elders we hear a new voice: "In trying to figure out how I see God, I found out a lot about myself. I found out I have a lot of anger, and at first I thought it was God's fault; but now I see the anger was with other people and with myself."

The woman sounded astonished, as though she were realizing for the first time that the knowledge of God and the knowledge of ourselves are "so intimately connected, which of them precedes and produces the other is not easy to discover."

The elder of Eternal God and the elder of Unknown Spirit shared the woman's astonishment. They were amazed that in trying to figure out how she saw God, the woman discovered a lot about herself. To understand their surprise, we have to go back to what the elder of Eternal God first said when she introduced her name for God: "My relationship to God is utterly different from all of my other relationships. When I come to church I want to hear about God who is greater and better than anything else or anyone else. That's why I picked out 'Eternal.' Nothing else is eternal, only God. Eternal God." That is a very important truth about God. If the church ever loses the sense that its "relationship to God is utterly different" from all of its other relationships, "it will turn into an Elks Club"[11] or a therapy group or a coffee klatch. But if "Eternal God" is the sole name of God, then God will be too far away to help us untangle the spider web soul. God may then come to seem, as God does for the elder of Unknown Spirit, beyond the stars and black holes. We need God close as well as far. We need Emmanuel, "God-with-us."

Simply preaching Christ will not give us Emmanuel. It is possible to portray Christ so that he seems as distant and unrelated to our self-discovery as Unknown Spirit or God the Vague. Rembrandt in his youthful career favored presentations of Christ that pictured him more as a hero than as the Savior.[12] For example, about 1632, Rembrandt did an etching of the raising of Lazarus that makes Jesus look like a magician. Jesus stands with his right side turned toward us. His right hand is on his hip and his face is turned so that we only get his profile, like that of a star from the silent movie era. His left arm is extended up into the air with the fingers open. At his feet we see Lazarus, waking as though from a hangover. Behind Jesus and to the right of Lazarus in the background are stunned spectators, one of them with his arms thrown open in utter shock. We can almost hear Jesus conjuring Lazarus from the dead with the wave of his left hand and an "abracadabra." The picture might be titled "How He Wowed Them in Bethany." There is more theater than theology in the picture. The artist's melodramatic Jesus is someone too removed from our humanity for us to discover something of ourselves through him.

But in 1642, Rembrandt did another etching of the raising of Lazarus, and like a preacher returning to the same text, the artist presented the truth of the gospel in an utterly new way. This time Jesus faces us. His hands are closer to his body and raised very gently, no higher than midchest. He does not loom over the spectators but stands among them. They look on as people who are almost participating, sharing in the miracle. And, oh, the face of Jesus! If we look closely, we notice that his eyelids are puffy. "Jesus wept," says the Gospel of John, and this time Rembrandt presents us with a Savior who has wept, someone who knows our pain.

"In trying to figure out how I see God, I found out a lot about myself," said the woman in the circle of elders. And in looking at the Savior with puffy eyelids, we discover a lot about ourselves, because this is a Lord who is connected to our humanity as well as to God. Christ's life begins to make sense out of our lives, because the image of Christ that Rembrandt presents hooks our images of ourselves. We come to see that Christ's humanity frees us to accept our own humanity.

Because Christ was tempted, we can acknowledge that we, too, are tempted.

Because Christ was betrayed and deserted, we can trust that God understands our loneliness when our friends let us down.

Because Christ suffered, we know God feels with us when we are hurt.

Because Christ was afraid to die, we can acknowledge the same fear in ourselves.

We are glad not only for how God became human in Christ but also for how God makes us human through Christ.

"In trying to figure out how I see God, I found out a lot about myself." The elder was sharing more than a passing insight. She was in touch with a fundamental dynamic of God's movement among us. She was in touch with what John Calvin put in words—that the knowledge of God and the knowledge of self are "intimately connected"—and she was in touch with what Rembrandt captured in the second etching.

What image of Christ does our preaching present? Is it the abracadabra Jesus or the Savior with the puffy eyelids? Is it God-

beyond-us or God-with-us? With us in joy. With us in sadness.
With us in life. With us in death.

The surgeon of our souls is not a robot who never bled himself.
Because Christ has experienced being human, we are willing to
risk our humanity in his hands. We may be suspicious of ma-
gicians, but someone who weeps with us in our grief calls forth
our trust. We are willing like the poet to climb down into Lazarus' grave and to be called forth to new life ourselves:

> All silence. Memory tries. More silence, and this will go on. Mem-
> ory is struggling. I am very cold. I am wrapped in something. I
> might be able to move. I am not able to try yet. I will not try.
> Maybe later. My mouth is full of dryness. It might be dust, it might
> be sand, or simply the taste of nothingness itself. I have been dead.
> But something is happening to me that all the dead long for.
>
> I smell the decay that is my own. My nose is underground. I
> can inhale, and what enters my lungs is the sweat of interior
> stones. But somehow the air is becoming sweet. Someone is tap-
> ping on thick stone. I hear a voice saying, "Come forth." Light
> strikes me full in the forehead and I open my eyes. Through the
> cloth over my head, I see a man of infinite gentleness come toward
> me crowned with new leaves. I cannot tell which is He, or which
> is the sun itself. A voice bids me to rise and come forth. I do, and
> I am alive.

Alive[13]

Read the passage again, this time aloud. Pause after each
period.

"All silence."

Be silent.

Be silent with the silence of Aud's husband going back to the
burned cabin and wandering down to the pond and looking
absently at his reflection.

Be still.

Be still with the stillness of death.

Be still with the stillness of all the deaths you have known.

Be still with the stillness that will be yours when you die.

Be still.

"Memory tries."

Let your memory strain to pull up the feeling of the time you
first fell in love, the first wave of desire, the first wave of wanting
to live your life for someone else, the first wave of wild, extrav-
agant, outlandish commitment and passion.

"More silence, and this will go on."

Stop remembering. Stop pulling up the waves of love.

Then let them continue.

Like Isabel Moore's grief, keep alternating them.

Silence, memory, silence, memory, silence, memory, silence, memory.

"Memory is struggling."

Memory is struggling to remember life:

Morning coffee.

Sunshine on the cedars and the maples.

The moisture of the first kiss.

Curling your toes in the sand at the beach.

"I am very cold."

Like on a February morning when I had to wear my nylon driving gloves because I left my woolen ones at a friend's. The joints are ice, ice picks, sharp, stiff, pointed, cold beyond recovery, cells of flesh as broken as tomatoes caught in the frost.

"I am wrapped in something."

A shroud, like a sleeping bag that is too tight for moving legs and arms.

"I might be able to move. I am not able to try yet. I will not try."

"Maybe later."

Only maybe. Not for sure. There is no sureness.

Or at least there is only sureness about my stillness, about my death.

"My mouth is full of dryness. It might be dust, it might be sand, or simply the taste of nothingness itself."

I have tasted it in this study when I spread out my books and commentaries on top of the pew cards from people who want me to visit and I cannot come up with a single idea. I have seen so much life and death, but they have left only dust in my mouth, no moist words, no ideas pliant with life, but only dust.

"I have been dead."

I have been like O. E. Parker who was content with merely existing until he saw the tattooed man at the fair.

I have been dead as Isabel's father, dead as Aud, her head kicked in by the crazed deer.

"But something is happening to me that all the dead long for."

Do not rush from this moment.

Find that point inside you from which life stirs:

the twine of the chromosome,

the filament of cells,

the center of the heart,

the soul.

Feel its force trilling in the blood.

"I smell the decay that is my own."

Smell, decay, sense, sense of smell.

"My nose is underground. I can inhale, and what enters my lungs is the sweat of interior stones."

All of my childhood fears in a single waft of air.

Being enclosed in a grave.

Suffocated by earth.

"But somehow the air is becoming sweet."

Not closed in?

An outer world greater than my grave?

"Someone is tapping on thick stone."

Tap, tap, tap,

Knock, knock, knock.

Beat, beat, beat.

"I hear a voice saying, 'Come forth.'"

I can get out?

I can get out!

"Light strikes me full in the forehead and I open my eyes."

The body that would not move can open its eyelids.

"Through the cloth over my head, I see a man of infinite gentleness come toward me."

The Savior with the puffy eyelids.

He has been weeping for me and his tears have made him close to me, and his tears have made him far from me because they were the tears of the living and I was dead. But now he brings his life to me.

"I cannot tell which is He, or which is the sun itself."

Life, breath, sight—all one dazzling light.

"A voice bids me to rise and come forth."

Lazarus, come out.

Isabel Moore, come out from your grief.

Elder of God the Vague, come out from your doubt.

Andrea Winston, come out from your self-hate.

Preacher in your study, come out from despair.

With a loud voice the Savior commands, "COME OUT."

"I do, and I am alive."

"Alive"

Alive with Christ, alive with life, alive with love. "Alive"

There is no period after the word because I am completing Lazarus' story with my story and because I am alive with everlasting life, life that ends with eternity rather than with a period. I am alive through the power of the Savior with the puffy eyelids. His humanity has led me to claim my humanity, and my humanity has in turn led me to listen to him as he calls me from underground, from "the sweat of interior stones," from my grave of fear and doubt.

A Sense of Self Through the Senses

How has the poet used words to call me into the presence of the Word who is life?

Note first what he has not done. He has not argued about the miracle. He has not opened with grand ruminations on our distance from the biblical witness: "Today's text is problematic for our scientific age." The poet grasps what New Testament scholars tell us: the gospel accounts are not straight history but the early church's expression of faith. The poet pulls on every faculty of understanding that we have:

We *hear:* "Someone is tapping on thick stone."

We *think:* "Memory is struggling."

We *feel:* "I am very cold."

We *taste:* "My mouth is full of dryness."

We *smell:* "My nose is underground."

We *see:* "Light strikes me full in the forehead and I open my eyes."

We *move:* "A voice bids me to rise and come forth. I do, and I am alive."

The entire person is engaged by the text. Not just the mind, not just the reason, not just the heart, but the whole human being. All of us is called forth for all of God. The poet realizes that the human self is not a chain of logic but a multi-layered reality in which the different levels of being and meaning are simultaneously engaged. The nose smells "the sweat of interior stones." At the plainest level of reality the olfactory organ is functioning. But what associations that single smell touches off: fear, dying, death, grave, burial, dark! All of these are stirred at a conscious or subconscious level by a single smell, "the sweat of interior stones." The poet does not have to argue us into a desire to hear Christ. We are ready, because from the surface to the depths of our being we yearn for the voice from beyond ourselves.

"A voice bids me to rise and come forth. I do, and I am alive." Our response flows out of the total experience rather than out of the force of some carefully reasoned position. This does not mean that the poet has abandoned reason. Twice he uses highly sophisticated mental constructions: "Memory is struggling" and "the taste of nothingness itself." But these ideas have weight and force precisely because they are interwoven with the sensuous and kinesthetic faculties.

The cold, the dust, the smell, the tapping, and the light are like a mooring buoy that I used in helping my father with our boat when I was a child. The buoy was attached to a large concrete anchor that lay on the bottom of our lake. During the summer the water level would sink and we needed to move the mooring farther from shore to keep our boat from going aground. Rather than dive to the bottom and struggle with the anchor itself, our family would all get in the sailboat at once and crowd in the bow until the front gunwhale was only an inch or two from the surface of the lake. We then tied the buoy into the boat, taking all of the slack out of the line. Next, we all moved to the stern of the boat, an action that now lifted up on the anchor so that it was a foot or two off the bottom. We paddled the boat to deeper water and then got back in the bow to let the anchor down in its new location. We had touched only the buoy on the surface, but we had moved the greater weight in the depths. And that is exactly what the poet does! He describes the sensuous world at the surface of our awareness in order to move the greater weight in the depths of our souls.

We preachers too often reverse the process. We try to move the anchor directly, and the result is that our language becomes pretentious and ponderous: "This morning I would like to talk about the fear of death that is part of the anxiety of being human." No! Move that buoy: "My nose is underground. I can inhale, and what enters my lungs is the sweat of interior stones."

Imagine if Jesus, on the night of his betrayal, had said, "Now, I want you all to remember me. Here are some important ideas that you should recall and tell one another about so that you will be true to who I am and what I have thought." Instead, Jesus gave them bread—the same stuff that children spread with peanut butter and jelly for lunch, bread like you will put in the toaster tomorrow morning, bread for the hungry, bread for the world. Jesus gives us a broken crust and hands us a universe of meaning. The poet wafts the smell of interior stones toward us and our souls get ready for Christ.

Next time you prepare a sermon, go through the notes with your nose. Do you smell anything?

Go through the notes with your body. Do you feel anything?

Go through the notes with your eyes. Do you see anything?

Go through the notes with your mouth. Do you taste anything?

Go through the notes with your ears. Do you hear anything?

Watch this last one. It is the trickiest. Of course, you will hear something, and, of course, your congregation will hear something—your voice! But will the congregation hear anything else? "Someone is tapping on thick stone."

Engaging the total person is more than poetry or sound communications technique. It is sound theology. "The marvel of man's bodily appearance is not at all to be excepted from the realm of God's image. This was the original notion, and we have no reason to suppose that it completely gave way, in P's [Priestley's] theological reflection, to a spiritualizing and intellectualizing tendency. Therefore, one will do well to split the physical from the spiritual as little as possible: the whole man is created in God's image." [14] The whole woman is created in God's image.

We are not redeeming God's cussing, killing beauties with our preaching if we are speaking only to a single aspect of who they are, if we split the physical from the spiritual and then speak only to the one but not the other. Preaching that appeals to the mind but never to body is unbiblical. ". . . you shall love the Lord your God with all your heart, and with all your soul, and with all your mind, and with all your strength" (Mark 12:30). To fulfill the first and greatest commandment requires connecting with the entire image of God. How we would like to wheedle out of this commandment. It would make living—and preaching!—much easier. We would like to say to God, "Let's be reasonable. You ask too much, Lord. I would gladly love you with all my heart if that were your only demand. I would have strong feelings about you and form the closest emotional ties with you and preach a heart-felt religion so long as you would leave the rest of me to myself."

Or "I would love you, God, with all my soul. I would become profoundly spiritual and pray and meditate for many hours and preach sermons to heal the sin-sick soul if you would not require all of me."

Or "I would love you, God, with all my mind. I would entertain great ideas about you and become a student of your Word and build sermons of impeccable logic and scholarship so long as you would not insist that the congregation's and my words become one with our actions."

Or "I would discipline my body and expend my strength in your mission and arouse the congregation to active service so long as we could keep our thoughts and feelings out of your realm."

Unfortunately our sermons sometimes sound as though God has listened to our argument and said, "All right, I'll settle for just your mind." But God has said no such thing. God demands the entire human being: heart and soul and mind and strength all together. And preaching that does not engage them all is more than poor communication. It is unfaithful to God. God wants the whole person, not just a piece.

To proclaim the fullness of God's demand requires that we preachers acknowledge it ourselves. We must experience the totality of God's image in us before we can engage it in others. The preacher with a truncated sense of self preaches a truncated gospel. Too often heart, soul, mind, and strength are separate cells within us. We only admit God to one room at a time because that is all we ever occupy ourselves. We are not even sure of the corridors that connect one vault to another. Sometimes we need to move from the heart to the mind but we are shackled by feeling; sometimes, from the mind to the heart but we are bound by thought; sometimes, from the body to the soul but we are chained by desire; sometimes, from the soul to the body but we are handcuffed by piety. There is no way we preachers will ever get free inside unless God shines in our own dungeoned darkness, and God is not going to shine if every time we get trapped, we try to ignore the predicament of our own lives by calling Arlot's Office Supply or drawing a new organizational chart.

> . . . . Our temples temple.
> From morning until night, frenetically,
> they go about the busy work of templing.
> And there's another reason why we can't
> authentically appropriate the vision:
> our minds are much too busy being minds,
> and much too noisy making thinking sounds.
> From morning until night, frenetically,
> we celebrate the work of cerebration.[15]

Whoever I Am

"All silence. Memory tries. More silence, and this will go on."

This will go on in Lazarus' tomb.

This will go on in the preacher's study.

"Memory is struggling." I am struggling to remember a poem about the self. The last line sticks in my mind and will not let me go: "Whoever I am, thou knowest, O God, I am thine." Thine, thine, thine, thine, thine. . . . The word paces up and down through my head. "Footfalls echo in the memory,"[16] and I hear voices of people to whom I must preach: "I am vague about God." God, God, God, God, God—the word, the need, the meaning reverberate in my head. "God seems way beyond the stars and the blackholes where I can never reach." Reach, reach, reach, reach, reach. . . . "She's a beauty and she doesn't see it." See it, see it, see it, see it, see it, see it. . . .

"Quiet!" I want the speakers to hold their peace and to listen to the poet and to believe what he says, because it is true for them and for me as well as for him: "Whoever I am, thou knowest, O God, I am thine." Thine, thine, thine, thine, thine. . . . But they will never believe it if I give that final line alone. It is the way the poet builds to the line that would capture their attention. He speaks the way they speak, not at all religious until the very end, but very convincing then. Thine, thine, thine, thine. . . . "Memory is struggling."

This study seems like a prison sometimes. "Whoever I am, ..." Prison! That's it! *Letters and Papers from Prison*. Bonhoeffer. Where is that book? Oh, why can't I find something when I need it? Here it is. Now where is the poem? I turn to the index. It must be under "Poems" or "Poetry." Here's *P*:

Participation
Passiontide (*see also* Easter)
Past, the
Pastor(s)
Pastoral care
Patience
Peace
Penal justice
Peritome
Philosophy
Pietism
Piety
Politics

Wait a minute. Where is "Poetry"? Maybe it got misplaced, typesetter's error.

Polyphony
Positivism of revelation (*see also* Karl Barth)
Power
Prayer

No, it's not misplaced. It's not here. But I know the poem is
in the book. I read it fifteen years ago, but it still sticks in my
mind. Bonhoeffer is in prison and all of these people are telling
him how happy he looks and he is baffled because he does not
feel all that great inside of himself. Why isn't it in the index?
Was it an oversight? No, it is not an oversight. It is blindness.
The worst kind: theological blindness. There is room for *"Peri-*
tome" and "Positivism of revelation," but there is no room for
"Poetry." That is not fair to Bonhoeffer. There was room for
poetry in his soul, good poetry. Here it is, fifteen years after I
read the book, and I still can tell you the outline of the poem
and a line I can't forget: "Whoever I am, thou knowest, O God,
I am thine."

Maybe the poem is in the table of contents. What was the
title? I scan down the page into Part 3 of the contents and read,
"The Past. A poem." That is not it, but I am glad to know that
poems are identified. Maybe there is hope for us theologians
after all.

WHO AM I? That's it! I flip excitedly to page 347. The poem
stands out from the prose. I read the first stanza:

> Who am I? They often tell me
> I would step from my cell's confinement
> calmly, cheerfully, firmly,
> like a squire from his country-house.

He sounds like the elder of Unknown Spirit walking with his
wife around their new place in the country.

> Who am I? They often tell me
> I would talk to my warders
> freely and friendly and clearly,
> as though it were mine to command.

The guts the man must have had! "Guten Morgan, Herr Com-
mandant. Wie geht's?"

> Who am I? They also tell me
> I would bear the days of misfortune
> equably, smilingly, proudly,
> like one accustomed to win.

Bonhoeffer has asked the question three times and not yet

mentioned God. He talks as people do when they are not being religious for the pastor or for church.

> Am I then really all that which other men tell of?
> Or am I only what I know of myself,
> restless and longing and sick, like a bird in a cage,
> struggling for breath, as though hands were compressing my
>   throat,
> yearning for colours, for flowers, for the voices of birds,
> thirsting for words of kindness, for neighbourliness,
> trembling with anger at despotisms and petty humiliation,
> tossing in expectation of great events,
> powerlessly trembling for friends at an infinite distance,
> weary and empty at praying, at thinking, at making,
> faint, and ready to say farewell to it all?

He has been praying, but there is still no sign of God in the poem. The prayers have gone unanswered. The elder of God the Vague can relate to that.

> Who am I? This or the other?
> Am I one person today, and tomorrow another?
> Am I both at once? A hypocrite before others,
> and before myself a contemptibly woebegone weakling?
> Or is something within me still like a beaten army,
> fleeing in disorder from victory already achieved?

Questions, questions—they go on and on, the way they do in the elders and in Peter Linden and in Isabel Moore.

> Who am I? They mock me, these lonely questions of mine.
> Whoever I am, thou knowest, O God, I am thine.[17]

At long last, "God." A single mention of God; yet fifteen years later I remember the impact of the line. Why? Because my humanity has been taken seriously, because God has not been dragged prematurely into every verse, because grace has not appeared quickly and cheaply, because Bonhoeffer has faced the struggle of the self honestly. When the final line comes, "Whoever I am, thou knowest, O God, I am thine," I feel released— like pressure off me, like an opening in a walled room, like a voice that "bids me to rise and come forth."

Bonhoeffer's psychological integrity makes his theological affirmation unforgettable. What if he had written the poem in reverse, repeating the line "Whoever I am, thou knowest, O God, I am thine" three times in the opening verses instead of "Who am I?" The power of the poem would have evaporated because we would not feel the struggle that gives the final creed meaning.

Unhistorical, Solitary, Guilty

"Who am I? They mock me, these lonely questions of mine."

They mock Dietrich Bonhoeffer, confined to his cell for plotting to overthrow Hitler.

They mock us preachers, confined to our own shriveled visions of who we are and what God can do with us.

But these lonely questions are a blessing as well as a curse. They are a blessing because, although they seem only to be mocking me, they are in fact mocking everyone else as well. These lonely questions form a bond between pew and pulpit. They mock Isabel Moore, confined to her grief for refusing to release its full fury, and they mock the elder of Unknown Spirit, confined to an impersonal God beyond the stars and the black holes, and they mock Andrea Winston, confined to a distorted self-image because "she's a beauty and she doesn't see it." These questions represent what we all hold in common, listener and preacher alike, "the modern consciousness, that thing Jung describes as unhistorical, solitary, and guilty."[18]

Unhistorical.

That's us all right. We can pull up a few dates from history—1066, 1492, 1588, 1776, 1864, 1929, 1945—and match them to the proper events on a multiple choice test, but we have no sense of what they have to do with us, how they have made us who we are, how they shape our understanding. Those lonely questions mock us because we see ourselves isolated in time. We are no longer like those ancient Israelites who knew who they were because they were connected to history: "And you shall make response before the LORD your God, 'A wandering Aramean was my father; and he went down into Egypt and sojourned there, few in number; and there he became a nation, great, mighty, and populous'" (Deuteronomy 26:5). We no longer have such a profound sense of being linked to the past as the Israelites, who found their identity in reciting these words about their forebears.

Solitary.

That is us, too. Eighteen elders sit in a circle struggling to figure out their image of God. They have hashed out the same budget, hired contractors to fix the same church furnace, even served the same Communion together, but when they begin to talk about how they see God and themselves, they are astounded at how distinctly different they are. One says to me privately, "We seem so separate, I begin to wonder if we even worship the same God." The solitariness of the modern consciousness pervades the sanctuary as well as the streets.

Guilty.

It is not just the guilt over things we did wrong or nasty thoughts or severe words. It is the guilt that Isabel Moore acknowledges to be her "worst sin" but that she cannot confess, "for the Church had not thought of a confessable name for it: the hunger of my spirit, the utter selfishness of my heart."[19]

"Who am I? They mock me, these lonely questions of mine."

Who are you, eighteen elders in your circle? Who are you, Andrea Winston in your studio? Who are you, preacher in your study? Are you not, like Flannery O'Connor, Christians "peculiarly possessed of the modern consciousness, that thing Jung describes as unhistorical, solitary, and guilty"? That is who I am. I love the Bible; I have been raised on its stories and I read it every morning, but I do not live in the Bible. I live now. I live here in this contemporary world, and I live in it with a modern consciousness—unhistorical, solitary, and guilty. Yes, I know that the battle of Hastings was in 1066, and the Spanish Armada was defeated in 1588, and the American Revolution was in 1776, but the past does not flow in my blood as it did for earlier generations. And yes, I love the church as a corporate body of believers, and often it rescues me from becoming completely solitary; but if I am radically honest, I can see that I live very much in my own head, my own heart, and my own self, like Isabel Moore. Don't you? And yes, I have heard the good news, "In Jesus Christ you are forgiven." I have heard it in hundreds and hundreds of worship services, but still something is not aright, something is not convinced inside of me. And when I stand in the pulpit and I look out at the faces of Peter Linden and Andrea Winston and the elder of God the Vague, I do not see people who live in the Bible either, but people who live now and in the same contemporary world and with the same modern consciousness—unhistorical, solitary, guilty. I am not talking about what they know intellectually. They know history and community and forgiveness. I am talking about the knowledge in their bones, the vision in the blood, the shape of the bulb of awareness. It is not the same as it once was.

I receive a medieval block-print Christmas card of the three wise men approaching the holy family through a gothic arch and I put it on the end table next to the newspaper, and I know the human consciousness that was in the past has cracked, broken, shattered, been swept utterly away. When I read the lesson, "the Word became flesh," it does not sound the same to me or to the congregation as it did to the artist who carved the block that made the print of the three noblemen stepping through a gothic arch to worship a cherubic infant.

"To possess this [modern consciousness] *within* the Church is to bear a burden."[20] It would be easier if we could put the burden down when we went to church, if we could run a notice in the newsletter: "Leave your modern consciousness at the kitchen table along with your half-finished coffee and come to a world of ancient times. There will be time enough for the modern consciousness when you return to read the Sunday paper." Or it would be easier if we forgot church altogether, if we decided that we would simply live with our modern consciousness, and if on Sunday morning we took time for the

> Complacencies of the peignoir, and late
> Coffee and oranges in a sunny chair. . . .[21]

But when we do, our minds drift

> Over the seas, to silent Palestine,
> Dominion of the blood and sepulchre.[22]

So we are stuck with them both together, the church and the modern consciousness. There is no escaping this truth for us preachers or for our listeners. To bear the modern consciousness within the church is "the necessary burden for the conscious [Christian]."[23] It is necessary because there is no other way that we can be both faithful to God and relevant to the contemporary world. To bear this burden steadily and honestly is "to feel the contemporary situation at the ultimate level."[24] It is to know that our cussing and our killing, our suffering and our begetting have a meaning that extends beyond the dimensions of our daily world. How will we preachers tell our people that? How will we declare a faith that is historical, corporate, and merciful to people whose consciousness is unhistorical, solitary, and guilty? Here is how we will do it.

Before we start trying to put words together, we will follow Flannery O'Connor into the spider web soul. We will lower ourselves with James Dickey into the grave. We will sit in jail with Dietrich Bonhoeffer. And while we are there, we will carry nothing with us, no preconceptions about right belief, no church position papers, no doctrines. When we have arrived in the center of the soul—at the smallest circle of the spider web, on the floor of the grave, in the cell of the prison—we will do nothing, except look out upon the world from the heart of darkness, seeing it with the eyes of unbelief, understanding it through the modern consciousness. We are not trying to get up a sermon, at least, not yet. We are trying to do something that comes before the sermon: getting in touch with the human soul that must receive our words. We cannot feed people what they do not hunger for, and we cannot appreciate their hunger if we have not known it ourselves. That is the secret of the power of Flannery O'Connor, James Dickey, and Dietrich Bonhoeffer; the same hunger is rumbling in them or their characters that is rumbling in the readers. They let transcendent truth emerge through a recognizable humanity. O. E. Parker gets thrown out of a pool hall brawl with liquor on his breath as thick as any other drunk's before he knows that the figure on his back is the Lord who commands obedience. The poet lies in the grave, still as any other corpse, before the voice calls to "come forth." Dietrich Bonhoeffer is tortured by the question "Who am I?" as persistently as any other lost soul before he claims, "Whoever I am, thou knowest, O God, I am thine."

The cherubic infant of the medieval Christmas card gives a warm glow to the season, but the recognizable humanity of O'Connor, Dickey, and Bonhoeffer wins from the modern consciousness a hearing for the transcendent truth of God. What do we preachers give our people? The block print of belief or a recognizable humanity that opens them to God?

Angel with an Orange Sword

I am tempted to walk through the gothic arch back into the past, back to a more innocent age, back to the Garden. I sit at the table in my kitchen on December 27. It is early and no one else is with me except the three wise men and the cherubic infant I have brought to the table to look at while I drink my coffee. Some wrappings are spread on the table and there is silence except that I hear

> Footfalls echo in the memory
> Down the passage which we did not take
> Towards the door we never opened
> Into the rose-garden. . . .[25]

. . . or into this courtyard with the cherubic infant lying on hay at his parents' feet. O God, why could faith not be simpler, easier, more comfortable! I listen again to the footfalls echoing and I see the three noblemen are walking toward the child, and the last one through the arch beckons me to follow and I do, being sure to duck my head so that I do not bump it on the doorway. But when I get inside the courtyard, the child is not there. I look beyond the empty manger, with the archway to my back, and I see another door, slightly ajar. I walk toward it, confident that the wise men and the cherubic infant will be there. But as I approach it, I become less clear who it is or what it is I am after. I am simply aware that "Other echoes/Inhabit the garden."[26]

Echoes of home.

Echoes of childhood.

Echoes disturbed up out of my depths by the story of a child born in the hay.

I open the door and I see a tree, the giant oak tree in the field next to the house in which I grew up. One February when it was minus twenty degrees Fahrenheit, I skied up to that tree and I looked at it against the sky and the snow, gaunt as a mackerel bone against the shore of our lake. And I wondered how that tree kept coming back to life every spring. How did it stand there in minus twenty degrees in its skeleton and still return as a green beauty every summer? I was a sophomore then and skeptical about God. But I remember that day in the steel cold I had a glimmer of faith: If God can make a tree green again, maybe God can give life to the dead. Then the wind blew and I went inside. But the place where the glimmer of faith had shone still seemed warm, warm like the coffee mug in my hand set down on leftover Christmas wrappings for a coaster.

I take a sip and think, *This is the first Christmas I cannot go back home.* My parents have sold the house and moved south. But I want to go home. I want to go back to the oak tree and feel the place that was warm at minus twenty degrees and see the pasture up on the mountain across from the lake. The farmer who lived there once called us on the phone when I was playing my flute outside in the summer on a still evening and asked me to play "Londonderry Air." And I can see the pasture and the tree so clearly that I almost stand up from the table to get my car keys and drive there, when an angel appears who is as real to me as the hay in the empty gothic courtyard and the oak tree and the pasture. I recognize the angel from an old picture Bible I grew up with as a child. The angel has an orange sword and is standing between a green, green forest and a brown plain toward which a man and a woman are fleeing.

"You can't go back home."

I hear the words. They jolt me with a charge of white-hot truth. After I hear them, I sit stunned. Then I taste the coffee that I have been sipping absentmindedly, and I feel my knee resting against the table leg.

Preacher, you can't go back home. You cannot go back to the block print of belief of a grander age of faith, and you cannot lead your people back there. Isabel Moore cannot go back to the time when her father was alive. The eighteen elders cannot go back to John Calvin's confident assumption that "no man can take a survey of himself but he must immediately turn to the contemplation of God." Peter Linden cannot go back to his bog and have it be only a pudding of mud in which to play. None of us can go back to the Garden, though God knows we would like to. Perhaps that is why God has posted the angel with the orange sword there: not to judge us with flame, but to protect us from wasting our energy by trying to recover a past that has vanished.

I get up from the kitchen table and drop the three wise men and the cherubic child into the large butternut bowl where they land amidst reindeer and white steepled churches by Currier and Ives. I look at all those cards. The people who sent them are like me: they want to go back home. But they can't go back. The angel said, "You can't go back home."

Where is home now?

O God, where is home now?

I go back to the kitchen and sit down and pour myself some more coffee. My mind is empty, except that periodically, like a swell from the sea on a day when no violent breeze is blowing, this question waves through me: "Where is home now?" Then the mind is again still water.

The wave.

Still water.

The wave.

Still water.

The wave.

Still water.

The wave.

Still water.

The wave—wait a minute. The wave is bearing something. A phrase is surfacing; some words are being dragged up from the bottom. "Lord, thou hast been our dwelling place in all generations." God is home! I can live in God in whom we live and move and have our being. I am at home in God, here and now. I cannot go back to the Garden, but I can be with God in this time and place.

I find a Bible underneath a cookbook and read Psalm 90. "Lord, thou hast been our dwelling place/in all generations" (v. 1): *all* generations, all those who lived before me, yes, even the three wise men in the gothic arch. They lived in you in their own way, even as I must live in you in the style of this age. I am connected to them by you, and I am connected to you by them, by the way they passed on the faith. I am historical.

"Thou turnest man back to the dust,/and sayest, 'Turn back, O children of men!'" (v. 3). Isabel Moore is not alone in her grief. I am not alone in mine. It is to all of us that you speak. I am not solitary. I am one with all women, all men, for all of us are " . . . like grass which is renewed in the morning:/in the morning it flourishes and is renewed;/in the evening it fades and withers" (vv. 5-6).

"Thou hast set our iniquities before thee,/our secret sins in the light of thy countenance" (v. 8). Guilty. The psalmist is like us, guilty. The psalmist's feeling is our feeling and the psalmist's prayer is our prayer: "Let the favor of the Lord our God be upon us . . ." (v. 17).

I sit down on the couch in the living room. My wife is up. I hear the water running. She comes in and looks at my face.

"Something happen to you?"

What do I tell her? "An angel with an orange sword visited me and gave me a message from God"? It is too early in the morning for that; so I simply come out of my daze and say, "Oh, good morning. I was just thinking."

Just thinking.

Just remembering.

Just dreaming.

Just weaving in and out of my life and the Bible and the modern consciousness and the impact of O'Connor and Dickey and Bonhoeffer. Just receiving an angel from God.

That is how it happens. Angels do not only come from heaven on high. They swim up from the bottom of the soul, paddling with their wings to the surface. That must have been what happened to Dietrich Bonhoeffer sitting in his cell writing "Who Am I?" The fervor and flesh of that poem did not simply appear in the time that it took Bonhoeffer to get it down on paper. That poem was taking embryonic form for years and years. The experience of ambiguity about his self-image goes back at least as far as Bonhoeffer's childhood:

One day in the first form, when the master asked him what he wanted to study, he quietly answered theology, and flushed. The word slipped out so quickly that he did not even stand up. Having the teacher's gaze and that of the whole class directed at him personally and not at his work, and being suddenly called upon to speak out like this, gave him such conflicting feelings of vanity and humility that the shock led to an infringement of ordinary class behaviour, an appropriate expression of the consternation caused by the question and the answer. The master obviously thought so too, for he rested his gaze on him for only a moment longer than usual and then quickly and amiably released him. . . .

The boy absorbed that brief moment deep into himself. Something extraordinary had happened, and he enjoyed it and felt ashamed at the same time. Now they all knew, he had told them. Now he was faced with the riddle of his life. Solemnly he stood there in the presence of his God, in the presence of his class. He was the centre of attention. Did he look as he had wanted to look, serious and determined? He was filled with an unusual sense of well-being at the thought, though he immediately drove it away, realizing the grandeur of his confession and his task. Nor did it escape him at that moment that he had caused the master a certain embarrassment, though at the same time he had looked at him with pleasure and approval. The moment swelled into pleasure, the class-room expanded into the infinite. There he stood in the midst of the world as the herald and teacher of his knowledge and his ideals, they all had now to listen to him in silence, and the blessing of the Eternal rested on his words and on his head. And again he felt ashamed. For he knew about his pitiful vanity. . . .

. . . What was the meaning of the curious, mistrustful, bored, disappointed, mocking eyes of his class-mates? Didn't they credit him? Didn't they believe in his honesty? Did they know something about him that he did not know himself?

Why are you all looking at me like that? Why are you embarrassed, sir? Look away from me, for heaven's sake, denounce me as a mendacious, conceited person who does not believe what he says. Don't keep so considerately silent, as if you understood me. Laugh aloud at me, don't be so abominably dumb—it's intolerable.

There is the throng. He stands in the midst of it and speaks, fervently, passionately. He corrects himself. A leaden silence lies over the throng, a dreadful, silent mockery. No, it cannot be. He is not the man they take him to be. He really is in earnest. They have no right to scorn me. They are doing him wrong, all of them. He prays.

God, say yourself whether I am in earnest about you. Destroy me now if I am lying. Or punish them all; they are my enemies, and yours. They do not believe me. I know myself I am not good.

But I know it myself—and you, God, know it too. I do not need
the others. I, I. I shall win. Do you see their consternation? I am
with you. I am strong. God, I am with you.

Do you hear me? Or do you not? To whom am I speaking? To
myself? To you? To those others here?

Who is it that is speaking? My faith or my vanity?[27]

Dietrich Bonhoeffer the child stands before his schoolmaster
and his classmates and wonders if he looks "as he had wanted
to look, serious and determined." Dietrich Bonhoeffer sits in his
cell and wonders, "Who am I? . . . Am I then really all that
which other men tell of?" A resilient filament of life and experience twists and curls from the schoolboy to the prisoner. "The
Child is father of the Man. . . ."[28] Our earliest years are mother
to our adult. Fictional writers have long known this. I believe
it was Joseph Conrad who said that childhood was the treasury
from which great writers draw. We preachers need to draw on
that treasury in our sermons. A sermon is not precisely like a
poem or a piece of fiction. It is different in this way: there is a
basic story in Scripture that is already recorded and is ours to
tell. But the best sermons are those in which the biblical message
has the vitality of our own life experience to give witness to the
authenticity of the message.

The preacher stands in the pulpit delivering a sermon to her
friend who is being ordained:

Tonight we celebrate the ordination of one of us, Doug Clark,
to the priesthood. Affirming the priesthood of all believers, as I
do, I believe that all of us as priests have come together to designate
one of our brothers as a priest, in no way different from us, except
inasmuch as tonight Doug is making a commitment to the priesthood as his vocation. All of us are priests, by baptism. Tonight
Doug will become a priest, by ordination, henceforth, marked by
his commitment to priesthood as central to his vocation, his profes-
sion, his life.[29]

From where does the conviction in her voice come? What are
the springs of her theology? Yes, of course, the Bible, the Ref-
ormation, the fundamental affirmation of the priesthood of all
believers. But there is more here. We see it in her eyes. We feel
it in the pace of the delivery. This truth drives from the toes up.
Why? What is the preacher in touch with that is fueling her
words with power? The answer is the same as for Bonhoeffer:
primary life experience. Let us go back in time for the preacher
as we did for the German poet-theologian. Listen to what the
preacher remembers in her own words:

Sophie Couch always wanted to be a priest. Perched in the apple tree, mischievously munching on green apples, she and I had many ponderous heart-to-hearts back when we were four or five.

"I'm gonna be a priest! Just like Mr. Burke."

"But Sophie!" I protested.

"It's what I'm supposed to be. I know it. I can feel it in my bones! I think in some funny sort of way I'm already a priest, and so are you."

"But Sophie, we're *girls!*" I insisted, wrinkling my brow and spitting out a seed for emphasis.

"So?" she queried.

The matter seemed simple to me, and closed. For Sophie Couch the matter was not closed. For her a matter was never closed or in any way definitive of who she was or who she might become. Sophie Couch was a young dreamer, a visionary, a child of far-reaching faith. Best of all, Sophie Couch was mine. She was my imaginary playmate, an extension of me, created to fill some of the relational gaps I experienced in being an only child for six years.

An imaginary playmate is a godsend. . . .[30]

A godsend! One-sent-by-God. A messenger. An angel with an orange sword. Angels swimming up from the bottom of the soul, paddling with their wings. Where are they swimming up in you? Are you giving them time to surface?

Read, yes.

Study, yes.

Write and rewrite, yes.

But for the love of God, daydream too. Let God speak to you through who you are—which is to say, through who you have been. If you don't, then God will not be able to speak through you to the congregation.

Do not go back through the gothic arch to the cherubic child on the hay. It is Christ in your life, Christ in your people's lives, Christ in this world whom we seek. Do not go back, because it will be death to you. It will be the angel with the orange sword. But do remember. Remember the classroom and the teacher asking what you wanted to study. Remember the oak tree at minus twenty degrees. Remember the playmate munching on green apples. Remember what you remember or what you don't remember but that you might remember if you struggled to remember.

"All silence. Memory tries. More silence, and this will go on."

It will go on and on. But if you listen in the silence, if your entire self has been engaged by hard study, if your mind is alive with the images and insights of art and theology and pastoral experience and ordinary life, then you will hear that "someone is tapping on thick stone." Someone is tapping with stories, tapping with experiences—sunlight on a skirt, a summer storm at the lake, fireflies at midnight—and through them all you hear a voice: "Come forth." You do, and you are alive, alive with Christ, alive with the Word of God, alive and ready to proclaim the truth! Alive

The Death of an Innocent Man

Out of the butternut bowl I pick up other Christmas cards at random. Three ships that look like the Nina, the Pinta, and the Santa Maria float out of a blue background with these words printed like waves beneath them: "I saw three ships come sailing." Then there is a Santa Claus who looks like the one Coca-Cola used to print on the back of the *Saturday Evening Post*. And there is a bold silk-screened Christmas tree on mottled brown paper. I turn to the back to see who printed it: "This card is printed on 100% recycled paper. No trees were killed to produce it." Save the trees. Save God's earth. Alleluia. Amen.

Next come the three wise men passing through the gothic arch, and then a great wild red falcon with hunters chasing it, all holding their bows fully bent in a stylized fashion, like ballet dancers in the *Firebird*. I turn it over. UNICEF. Oh, the children! Not the cherubic infant, but the starving children, the bleeding world, Christ among the least of our sisters and brothers. In a flash all the other images evaporate and words rumble up in my soul that I had almost forgotten: "I was hungry and you gave me food, I was thirsty and you gave me drink, . . . I was in prison and you came to me" (Matthew 25:35-36). And the words reshape everything else that I have written. They point to that unhistorical, solitary, and guilty consciousness with which we have been trying to connect and remind us not to get sucked into it ourselves. Go into the smallest circle of the spider web soul and into Lazarus' grave and into the innermost prison cell. But in trying to understand the heart of darkness, do not forget the world of darkness. See how darkness flows from one to the other: Not only does darkness flow from the heart into evil acts, but also in the other direction, darkness from evil acts into the heart. The beaten child, the starving mother, the tortured prisoner—darkness crowds into their hearts not from within but from without. Not all evil is born in the heart. A lot of it is crammed there against the wishes of the recipients. The minority child does not request prejudice; the political prisoner does not ask for the cattle prod.

"The artist has dedicated his services to the production of this card that all proceeds might go to the United Nations Emergency Relief Fund."

I turn the card back over to look at the great wild red falcon surrounded by the hunters still poised to shoot. When I first picked it up, I wondered why anyone would send it for a Christmas card; but now it strikes me as the most faithful greeting in the entire bowl of Santas and reindeer and shepherds and wise men and holy families. Who is the holy family anyway? Is it the medieval trio of halo-clad mother, child, and father sitting in the block print and staring up at me from the bottom of the butternut bowl? Or is it the family for whom the artist painted the great wild red falcon, the family of the starving and the sick? Or is it the church family I will preach to on Sunday—Isabel Moore and Peter Linden and the eighteen elders and Andrea Winston? Or is it the artist's own family, who will have a little less money this season because there will be no commission for the red bird? The holy family is all of these. But I will not get to preach to the entire family, only part of it. So I will have to speak to their consciousness while keeping in mind the other members of the holy family whom they may have forgotten. I will have to preach the way Bonhoeffer wrote from prison, speaking to his own family in their own terms about their own pain, yet never oblivious to the pain of others. One day he writes: "Some of the younger prisoners seem to have suffered so much from the long solitary confinement and the long dark evenings that they have quite gone to pieces."[31] And the next day his words are about his own family's suffering: "Of course, you, Maria and the family and friends, can't help thinking of my being in prison over Christmas, and it's bound to cast a shadow over the few happy hours that are left to you in these times. The only thing I can do to help is to believe and know that your thoughts about it will be the same as mine, and that we shall be at one in our attitude towards the keeping of this Christmas."[32] Bonhoeffer's zeal for the world is backed by an authentic human intensity that arises from his personal experience. His concern for others does not sound haughty or paternalistic, because it is connected to an acknowledgement of the suffering in his own family's life. Pastor and prophet are one integrated human being.

I pick up the great wild red falcon and open the card so that it stands on the drop-leaf table. I place next to it the three wise men and the cherubic infant. I look from the bird to the infant and from the infant to the bird. I wonder, from where did that bird come? Did he swim up from the depths, paddling with his wings? Did he swoop down from heaven like the dove that descended upon Jesus, wet from the Jordan? That red bird came from both places. He came from the creative center of the artist and he also came from the dominion of love. "The artist has dedicated his services to the production of this card that all proceeds might go to the United Nations Emergency Relief Fund." The great wild red falcon is the sacred dove, the Holy Spirit coming through the artist's work, coming through the eyes and the hand, coming through the paint and the canvass, the print and the paper, coming through the creation of love. The inner consciousness of the artist has gotten entwined with the consciousness of grace. If this can happen to the artist, it can happen to the preacher. I stare at the picture longer. I let it take control of me the same way I let a biblical text take control of me. I experience the color of the bird.

Red.
Wild red.
Scarlet red.
Vermilion red.
Blood red.
Blood?!
Whose blood?
The bird's blood.
Love's blood.
Christ's blood.

The picture exhausts me. I throw it down into the butternut bowl and I pick up the three wise men passing through the gothic arch to the cherubic child. The bird looks up at me from the bowl with its unwinking eye. I turn away and the bird descends upon me from heaven.

SWOOSH!

SPIRIT!

Quick now, here, now, always—
Ridiculous the waste sad time
Stretching before and after.[33]

Actually, it is not "waste sad time," but simply less intense time, time for reflection and study, time to order the ink for the mimeograph and to gather the reports for the annual meeting and to enjoy the fact that the Christmas pressure is off for now. The Spirit came to me, looking at that card, and all kinds of things flashed to the surface, but they have sunk back down inside me. That is all right. I let them resettle in me. They will form some new pattern. Meanwhile I keep reading and studying, and every now and then I take out the card and look at it. I know some sermons are forming inside of me. I cannot tell you what they are yet. But their genetic code is unfurling inside of me. I will still have to use the commentaries and I will struggle mightily to come up with a clear outline. But for now I will not force the sermons to the surface. Instead, I reread about Bonhoeffer's final days; and while I read, I keep in the back of my mind this question: How can I draw people out of their solitude, their historical isolation, and their guilt so that they will do justice, love mercy, and walk with God?

A doctor who witnessed Dietrich Bonhoeffer's execution, but did not know at the time who the poet-theologian was, later described his death in these words:

On the morning of that day between five and six o'clock the prisoners, among them Admiral Canaris, General Oster . . . and *Reichsgerichtsrat* Sack were taken from their cells, and the verdicts of the court martial read out to them. Through the half-open door in one room of the huts I saw Pastor Bonhoeffer, before taking off his prison garb, kneeling on the floor praying fervently to his God. I was most deeply moved by the way this lovable man prayed, so devout and so certain that God heard his prayer. At the place of execution, he again said a short prayer and then climbed the steps to the gallows, brave and composed. His death ensued after a few seconds. In the almost fifty years that I worked as a doctor, I have hardly ever seen a man die so entirely submissive to the will of God.[34]

Bonhoeffer's death calls up in me the deaths of millions and millions of innocent people gassed, shot, bombed, starved. I am numbed, almost incredulous at the capacity for evil that lies within us cussing, killing beauties. I return to the passage on Bonhoeffer and consider the death of this single individual. It is not that I am unconcerned about the millions, but that I cannot comprehend the terror; and my inability to comprehend leaves me less engaged than the solitary picture of one person's death. I have discovered that this is also the case with many others. It is not their lack of compassion but something else, some automatic defense system in the psyche, some survival mechanism in the nerves. Susan Sontag captures the reaction. She recalls seeing some photographs of the death camps, Bergen-Belsen and Dachau, in a bookstore:

> Nothing I have seen—in photographs or in real life—ever cut me as sharply, deeply, instantaneously. . . . When I looked at those photographs, something broke. . . . something is still crying.
>   To suffer is one thing; another thing is living with the photographed images of suffering, which does not necessarily strengthen conscience and the ability to be compassionate. It can also corrupt them.[35]

What Sontag says of photographs is also true of sermons. The preacher can corrupt the ability to be compassionate by overwhelming the congregation with the images of evil. In the face of incomprehensible brutality our modern consciousness puckers more tightly into itself, becoming more solitary, more unhistorical, and more guilty, until we are too paralyzed to act.

I return to the image of Bonhoeffer not to forget the masses of good people who died and are still dying, but to move beyond my defenses. " . . . I have hardly ever seen a man die so entirely submissive to the will of God," the doctor wrote. The death of a good man, the death of an innocent man, the death of a godly man—these simple phrases take shape in my head. I can hear someone saying them. I imagine myself in a courtroom, and I hear the prosecutor speaking: "We are gathered here today because an innocent man has been killed. He was a just man, a righteous man, a good man."

I hear the words and I see red—red like the great wild falcon who flies up from the depths after being submerged for several weeks and carries to me a message: Christ's blood. That's it! I have the sermon. Christ is the innocent man who has been killed. Yes, Bonhoeffer was the victim—and the millions of women and men who were innocent and who were killed and who are being killed—all are victims. But it is through Christ's death that I can engage the congregation's response to the other acts of injustice.

The sermon will be in a courtroom. It will be a trial. There is good precedence for it in the Old Testament. The prophets often call the people into the courtroom to make their case before God:

Set forth your case, says the LORD;
  bring your proofs, says the King of Jacob.
                                    —Isaiah 41:21

Let all the nations gather together,
  and let the peoples assemble.
Who among them can declare this,
  and show us the former things?
Let them bring their witnesses to justify them,
  and let them hear and say, It is true.
                                    —Isaiah 43:9

I sit in my study and feel like a prophet assembling the witnesses and preparing the case. On Sunday I step into the pulpit with a single prop, a mallet, which I bang three times and then announce to the congregation: "The court of inquiry is now in session. We have summoned you here today because an innocent man has been killed. He was a just man, a righteous man, a good man. Our task this morning is to get the facts straight, to find out who was actually responsible for the man's death.

"Four cryptic briefs have been submitted by Matthew, Mark, Luke, and John. They reveal that this man had a profound concern for others. All four show that he was completely innocent. His death was murder masquerading as justice. But today we shall get to the bottom of it. We shall discover who the guilty party is.

"I call first to the stand the wife of Judas Iscariot."

A woman comes forward and sits on a chair near the pulpit, facing out toward the congregation. We have taped cue cards to the little divider between the front pew and the chancel.[36] Again I speak as the judge.

"Down through the ages it has generally been held that your husband was responsible for the death of Jesus of Nazareth. Is that not true?"

Judas' wife starts slowly and tremulously, but later achieves the confidence of a woman who wants to clear her husband's name.

"That is what is thought. Yes, that's what is thought by many. But they're wrong; they've failed to read the Gospels closely. It's true enough that my husband did betray Jesus, but he did not kill him! Once my Judas saw his mistake, he did everything in his power to get Jesus free. You can read it in Matthew's account: how my husband returned to the priests, gave back the money, and pleaded with them. He pleaded that Jesus was innocent. He did. He did."

Scanning the congregation, Judas' wife continues: "You who are gathered here today must understand. My husband was a man of passion, a man who wanted to do the right thing no matter what the cost. That's why he joined the disciples in the first place. Oh, how I remember his coming home that first day!" Judas' wife focuses less on the congregation and begins to talk more to herself, like someone who is recalling a story of great personal meaning.

"My husband's eyes were blazing and there was new power in his husky voice. He said he'd found a good man, a man you could trust, a man the whole world could trust. My Judas said he had no other choice but to follow him. It would mean hardship for us as a family, but it was the right thing to do. And when Judas saw what he thought was right, well then, there was no stopping him.

"It was the same story when Judas betrayed Jesus. Judas did it because he thought Jesus had forgotten his original cause. Judas became convinced that he'd been wrong about Jesus. Yet, no sooner had Judas turned Jesus in, then he pleaded for him back. Can't you see? Can't you understand? There's a pattern to it all."

Judas' wife shakes her head, then stands up with anger and obvious disdain for the congregation. "Before you judge Judas, judge yourselves. Maybe Judas was impetuous, but at least he had a passion for what is right. Are you passionate for what is right? For what is just? Or are you neither hot nor cold but only lukewarm? Would you offer back a small fortune if you found out that it had been earned at the expense of justice? Don't ever forget this: my husband returned the cash, only Caiaphas and his cronies would not take the money in exchange for Jesus. They're the guilty ones!"

Then in a softer tone, but with intensity, Judas' wife thrusts her final words toward the congregation: "And remember this too: my husband gave back more than the money. My husband, Judas, gave back his life!"

I speak. "The first witness is dismissed." There is silence while Judas' wife makes her way back into the congregation and sits down in the pew next to Isabel Moore. Then I announce, "The court calls to the stand Caiaphas, the high priest who presided at the trial of Jesus."

Caiaphas comes forward. A well-dressed, comfortably situated man, he takes his time and sits down in the chair with an air of authority. I address him. "Honorable Caiaphas, you have heard the charge made by Judas' wife that you refused to take back the money and to acknowledge Judas' claim that Jesus was innocent. Furthermore, the briefs claim that false witnesses were allowed to testify. If this is true, then there has been a vast distortion of justice."

Caiaphas responds in the tone of one who is not used to being questioned. Although he raises his voice very little, we sense an anxious, nervous person underneath his calculated coolness: "Come now, let us not resort to inflammatory language. This man's death was no 'vast distortion of justice.' His death was the only reasonable course of action open to me and my colleagues. You must understand the complexities, the ambiguities that confront someone in my position. Integrity in a public office is never simple. Take, for example, your charge of false witnesses. To be sure, there were some individuals whose testimony was not precisely clear. But what is the lack of a little clarity when you balance it against what a dangerous man this Jesus was? He was a rabble-rouser, a threat to our tradition, our institutions, our whole way of life. He held model citizens up to the scorn of the common people and praised derelicts, cheats, whores, and other scum, simply because they trusted him. The man's behavior tore at the very fabric of society. There is no question about it; he was a dangerous man.

"Ask these people to the stand." Caiaphas points to the entire congregation. "They'll understand about the so-called false witnesses. They know what it is to have to cut corners with their integrity. We all do it: the doctored expense account, the tidbit of gossip told to reflect well on us, the lie of an official to protect our national defense. I do not think of those who spoke at Jesus' trial as 'false witnesses' but rather as 'guardians of the public good.'

"Besides, if you really want to question who was responsible, you should speak with Pilate. After all, we were not able to do anything with Jesus until it had been confirmed by Pilate. He had the final authority to let us proceed with the execution, an execution that, I would remind you, saved us from a dangerous man. Pilate should be praised, not cursed, for his courage in bringing the affair to its painful but necessary conclusion. Speak to him if you have any further questions."

Caiaphas gets up and leaves without waiting to be dismissed. He obviously considers the matter settled and has no intention of answering any more questions. He sits down in a pew behind the elder of Personal Jesus and in front of the elder of God the Vague.

I now speak reflectively, baffled by this new twist in the proceedings: "I had not planned on this. Pilate seems so quiet in the briefs. He is not bitter with Jesus. He encourages Jesus to defend himself. Indeed, at several points Pilate seems put off by the whole sordid business. He even disassociates himself by washing his hands of the affair. We shall see.

"The court calls Pontius Pilate to the stand."

Pilate comes forward and sits down with the energy of a man of action. His demeanor is of someone who gets through the business of life without getting bogged down in speculation about the finer points of religion and conscience.

"I find it incredible that I am called here. I have always been a good citizen. I have come up through the ranks. I served my country in the military. I was dependable and law-abiding. I earned my way to the top. After all the effort I put into my career and all the service I paid the state, I could not risk ruin for a Nazarene carpenter. Even the natives had a saying: 'Could anything good come out of Nazareth?' Who was I to argue with the man's own people?"

The constant repetition of "I" in Pilate's speech is a deliberate device to capture the solitude of the modern consciousness, the self-made person of American society.

I interrupt Pilate: "The question is, Was it in your power to prevent the death of this innocent man?"

Pilate evades the question. "You must understand my position. To set the man free was not the popular thing to do. The crowd was against him and the religious authorities were against him. They all agreed he had to be eliminated. Look, I admit I did not like the mess any more than you did. The man seemed innocent enough to me. He was a fool, but an innocent fool. I didn't see any harm he had done. Still, I could not risk a riot or Rome would have had my neck. It was that simple. I had to keep the peace."

I stop him again. "I ask you once more: Did you have the power to save this man from death?"

Pilate is silent, then begins to answer in a halting manner, "Well, I suppose if you look at it from one perspective, some people might conclude that the way the case was going it might have been. . . ."

I interrupt again, this time with anger and impatience. "Did you have the power?"

Pilate responds, "Well, yes, I guess you could say I had the power. I was the top authority."

I press on. "So you are the guilty one! The silent one. The one who couldn't get involved. The one who washed his hands of the whole affair. You were the one person who had the authority—the legal, political, and civil authority—to save this innocent man; yet you lacked the moral authority. You had the power, but you lacked the will!"

Pilate explodes in his own defense. "All right, all right, I was the one. But why do you stand there blaming me for an act of past history. Don't limit your conviction to me. Blame these people, too." Pilate stands up and gestures toward the entire congregation, at Isabel Moore and the lady of smooth-skinned, athletic Jesus and Peter Linden and the eighteen elders and Andrea Winston. Then he points at me. "Blame yourself. Christ is crucified daily and what do you do? Christ is crucified wherever people starve, wherever they are exploited and oppressed, and how do you respond? Do you just turn off your television or put down your newspaper and thank God that your own life goes all right? I tell you, I am no guiltier of Christ's death than any human being who sees injustice and does not act to stop it. Before you stick the guilt on me, take yourself into the divine court of justice and look into your own hearts."

There is a moment of silence. Then I tell Pilate softly and without any trace of special authority, "You may go." When Pilate is seated among the members of the congregation, I say, "You have heard Pilate's words. It is clear that the last witnesses to be called to the stand are you and I. So, then, let us draw near to heaven's throne and bring our case to the Divine Judge in prayer." And then all of us, all of us people lost in our solitude, lost in our historical isolation, lost in our guilt, pray together a unison prayer that I have written as part of the entire sermon, for the sermon is not yet over.

Our God and our Judge, we stand indicted before you:
    For failure to show compassion.
    For failure to do justice.
    For failure to protect the rights of others.
How do we plead, guilty or innocent? That is your question.
We plead extenuating circumstances.
We would have been compassionate, but we lacked the time and energy.

We would have done justice, God, but it would have endangered our own lives.

We would have protected the rights of others, except it interfered with our interests.

Heavenly Judge, step down to earth. Understand these things from our perspective.

Still your question persists: "Guilty or innocent?"

O God, guilty!

Your justice squashes every excuse, and your judgment condemns every alibi.

We stand guilty.

We have not been compassionate.

We have not done justice.

We have not protected the rights of others.

Yet before you pass sentence, we enter this last plea:

That you our judge will be our Savior.

That with a forgiveness we have never shown, you will pardon us.

That instead of locking us in the prison of guilt, you will free us to keep your law of love and justice.

We throw ourselves on the mercy of the court.

We trust not our goodness but your power to pardon and make us new.

This plea we enter through our only counselor and advocate, Jesus Christ. Amen.

People look up very slowly from the prayer. We are not solitary now. We feel our corporate failure. We are not unhistorical now. We sense the connection between the cross and the evening news. But we are still guilty, heavy with the sense of sin, burdened with St. Paul's knowledge of having left undone what he should have done. And every face that looks at me asks the same question: What happens with people who have sinned this deeply? And as I look at their faces, I hunger with them for the weight to be removed. I step down from the pulpit into the congregation, and in a voice that is hushed by the awareness of my own inadequacy, I tell them: "Hear now God's verdict on us all. In the name of Jesus Christ, you and I are forgiven."

Several people sigh. Everybody hears it, and they begin to smile. But it is clear that it is not just the sighs that made them smile. It is the good news of forgiveness. And it is so good and so wonderful that I cannot resist repeating it. So I do. Only this time my voice is much brighter and stronger than the first time, because now the burden is gone; and I can see people smiling and some of them crying with joy, and I say in a voice even louder than the one I used against Pilate, "In the name of Jesus Christ, we are forgiven. We are forgiven! Tell one another that. Turn to your neighbors and tell one another that in the name of Jesus Christ you are forgiven, and give one another the peace of God."

And they do, the entire congregation. Judas' wife tells Isabel Moore that she is forgiven, and Isabel Moore tells Judas' wife that she is. Caiaphas shares the good news with the elders of Personal Jesus and God the Vague, and Peter Linden and Pilate tell each other God has forgiven them. Peter is not quite sure that he follows the whole thing, but he likes how happy the adults are and the fact that they are talking to one another with as much joy as he and his friends at a birthday party; and, of course, Peter is absolutely right to think this, because it is a birthday party. The whole congregation is being born again, and it is time to be glad and to sing a song and we do. The organist launches right into it, and many people sing without even looking at their hymnbooks. They know the words by heart, and today they know the feeling in their hearts. The hymn puts in place whatever pieces of the truth fell between the cracks of the preaching and the praying:

> Amazing grace!
> How sweet the sound,
> That saved a wretch like me!
> I once was lost, but now am found,
> Was blind, but now I see.

Amazing grace saved Flannery O'Connor from getting sucked into her modern consciousness.

Amazing grace called the poet out of Lazarus' tomb.

Amazing grace kept Dietrich Bonhoeffer from playing it safe within the established church and his prominent family.

Amazing grace stirred the artist to paint his great wild red falcon and give it to UNICEF.

Amazing grace removes the blindness of our solitude, our historical isolation, our guilt.

But for amazing grace to work its wonders through a sermon, the preacher must be willing to go deep, deep down into the spider web soul. John Calvin arrived there when he reflected that the knowledge of God and the knowledge of ourselves "are so intimately connected, which of them precedes and produces the other is not easy to discover," and the woman in the circle of elders beheld the very core of her identity when she realized that "In trying to figure out how I see God, I found out a lot about myself." This innermost circle of the spider web soul is the heart of darkness where we breath the sweat of interior stones and where we are pursued by the question "Who am I?" If we preachers can clear away the tangled growth that covers the spot, then the great wild bird of the Holy Spirit can swoop with red grace into the midnight soul, and our listeners shall affirm for themselves, "Whoever I am, thou knowest, O God, I am thine." And having acknowledged God's claim, they can shake hands with us at the church door and go into the world to love mercy and to do justice and to walk humbly with God.

4

Dark-Rooted Language Under Speech

I am in my study looking up the lessons for Pentecost Sunday in the lectionary. 1 Corinthians 12:4-13. *"Varieties of gifts, but the same Spirit."* Overworked, I think to myself. Acts 2:1-13. It is a favorite text that I have not read in a long time. I turn to it and begin to read: "When the day of Pentecost had come, they were all together in one place. And suddenly a sound came from heaven like the rush of a mighty wind, and it filled all the house where they were sitting. And there appeared to them tongues as of fire, distributed and resting on each one of them" (vv. 1-3). Fire! Red.
Wild red.
Scarlet red.
Vermilion red.
Blood red.

SWOOSH!

SPIRIT!

The great wild bird descends from heaven and the air in my study thickens with the Holy Presence, and the flutter of sacred wings flaps a litany out of my brain:

Is this the fire that Moses saw?
Yes, this is the flame that burned in the bush and called the slaves to freedom.
Is this the fire that led by night across the desert wastes?
Yes, this is the flame that showed the way to the Promised Land.
Is this the fire that burned in Jeremiah's bones?
Yes, this is the flame that made the prophet rage with justice.
Is this the fire Isaiah saw that blazed with holiness?
Yes, this is the flame that cleansed his lips and sent him to the people.
Is this the fire that shines within our own deep hearts?
Yes, this is the flame that burns within us with faith and hope and love.

From where did this litany come?

It came from the color red. It came from last Christmas, from picking up the UNICEF card and experiencing the image whose meaning was not yet clear to me. The bird flew into me and stirred up all those Bible stories that I have been reading for years and years, not because I was going to be preaching on them but because they make up "the greatest treasure-house of powerful, disturbing, life-enhancing images in the whole of humanity's long history." I go into that treasure-house every morning to feel that power, to be disturbed, to have my life enhanced. I go without a thought of what will be in Sunday's sermon. I go to listen. I go to see for myself. I go to be remade. I go because God is there and *I* need God as much as anyone to whom I will ever preach. I go every day. I cannot say that every day is rewarding. Sometimes it is boring and tedious and everything seems faded and worn out from too much exposure, and the air seems musty with stale truth. But I still go prowling around through that treasure-house, because I know that what does not speak to me immediately may speak to me later. That is what is happening right now as the great wild red falcon flaps its wings and stirs up visions of breath and flame, visions from the Bible and visions outside of it.

"The choice is between fire and fire." Fire or fire, fire or fire, fire or fire. The line of a poem flickers in my mind. I have no trouble locating the piece, because it is from the same "Four

Quartets" section that floated into my memory when I was following the wise men through the gothic arch "Down the passage which we did not take/Towards the door we never opened." That is the associative connection in my psyche: the wise men, the bird, and the poem all entered my head at the same time, and now the lectionary text is calling them forth in a new pattern. I go to the bookcase and take down *The Complete Poems and Plays* by T. S. Eliot. Aha, here it is. It is better than I remembered:

> The only hope, or else despair
> Lies in the choice of pyre or pyre—
> To be redeemed from fire by fire.[1]

We must decide what will burn within us—"the choice of pyre or pyre." I return to the Acts text and read how the early church was redeemed from fire by fire, how the Holy Spirit gave the disciples the power to speak so that people from all nations dwelling in Jerusalem could understand them.

Next I turn to the Gospel, John 14:15-26. I always read every lesson. Even if I do not use them all, I need them to be reverberating inside me to bring up associations and insights that might otherwise be lost to my consciousness. I read the first three verses of the text: "If you love me, you will keep my commandments. And I will pray the Father, and he will give you another Counselor, to be with you for ever, even the Spirit of truth, whom the world cannot receive, because it neither sees him nor knows him; you know him, for he dwells with you, and will be in you" (vv. 15-17). I become aware that someone is looking over my shoulder. I turn around and who is there but the elder of Unknown Spirit. It is two o'clock on Tuesday afternoon and naturally the elder of Unknown Spirit is at his own desk in his own office, but he is also right here with me, looking over my shoulder.

I can hear the man plain as day: "God seems very distant, beyond the stars and the black holes where I can never reach." And I can picture his eyes scanning this last verse along with me and breaking it into two parts: the first half describes how the elder feels about God, "the Spirit of truth, whom the world cannot receive, because it neither sees him nor knows him," and the second half says what the elder is aching and yearning to experience, "you know him, for he dwells with you, and will be in you."

Because the elder is right there in the office with me, I find

I cannot skim over the words and take them at face value. That elder won't let me get away with any glib theology. That elder asks again the same question he asked in the circle at the retreat: "How can I feel closer to God?"

I tell the elder I will get back to him in a while, and I scribble a note and verse number down: "v. 17—elder of Unk. Sp. wonders how this is true."

I have got to finish reading the text. So I start to read the next verse, although I have the feeling that the elder has not budged an inch. He is there reading the same words with me: "I will not leave you desolate; I will come to you. Yet a little while, and the world will see me no more, but you will see me; because I live, you will live also" (vv. 18-19).

Now somebody else is looking over my other shoulder. Isabel Moore. She does not say a thing. She doesn't have to. I just look at her face and that says it all. "If I wasn't going to be left desolate, why did Dad die? Why do I feel like this? How can I ever find again the sureness I once had?"

I scribble another note: "vv. 18-19, Isab. M."

"In that day you will know that I am in my Father, and you in me, and I in you" (v. 20). Andrea Winston's husband squeezes between Isabel and the elder, and I hear him saying to both of them, "She's a beauty and she doesn't see it." And the text confirms it; God and Christ and ourselves, we are all inside one another somehow, but Andrea does not see it. I write another note: "And. W.—image of Christ within us."

I will never use all of these notes. But they will help me later. I will read them back to myself and try to listen to the sermon the way the congregation will hear it.

"He who has my commandments and keeps them, he it is who loves me; and he who loves me will be loved by my Father, and I will love him and manifest myself to him" (v. 21). No one new appears at my back. There are not a lot of people who have been asking about commandments that they have to keep. But I am aware of someone there in the room, hovering just above me, not weighing me down but lightening my load. "I have hardly ever seen a man die so entirely submissive to the will of God." Bonhoeffer! I look up for a second and hear an organ and a choir and congregation in full voice: "For all the saints who from their labors rest . . . !"

"Judas (not Iscariot) said to him, 'Lord, how is it that you will manifest yourself to us, and not to the world?' Jesus answered him, 'If a man loves me, he will keep my word, and my Father will love him, and we will come to him and make our home with him'" (vv. 22-23). "You can't go back home." I hear the angel with the orange sword speak again the words that were the text for my New Year's sermon. I picture once more the three wise men beckoning me beneath the gothic arch, but they fade quickly because I know that I don't have to go backwards to go home. Christ makes his home with me.

"He who does not love me does not keep my words; and the word which you hear is not mine but the Father's who sent me" (v. 24).

"Father. How many times does the word appear in this lesson?" The speaker is the elder of Tender Mother, who said in the circle of eighteen elders, "I never felt the warmth of my faith until I realized that I could speak to God the same way I used to speak to my mom when I was tiny and hurt." Her words called to mind Jeremy Brown, a kindergarten boy to whom I tried to teach the Lord's Prayer. I have always treasured the first words of the prayer because I carry within me an image of my own father coming into my bedroom and holding me when I was little. I can still see the door opening and the light from the hall and my father picking me up and walking back and forth in the room. As I was teaching the Lord's Prayer to Jeremy, I am sure my voice and eyes must have been intense with belief, because the opening words blend together in a single phrase my conviction and my primary life experience. I had gotten no further than "Our Father, who art in heaven," when I realized that Jeremy looked terrified. I stopped to find out what was wrong. "You mean God's like a father?" It was clear that "father" was such a profound stumbling block that there was no way Jeremy could proceed. It later came out from an older sister that his father had beaten Jeremy with a two-by-four and the court had moved the boy into the home of an aunt who was now raising him with love and affection. The youngster did finally learn the Lord's Prayer, but with these words: "Our Aunt, who art in heaven. . . ."

By now my study is very crowded. The great red falcon is flapping its wings. The elder of Unknown Spirit, Isabel Moore, Andrea Winston's husband, the elder of Tender Mother, and Jeremy Brown are bunched around my desk, looking down at Sunday's Gospel lesson, hungering for the truth that will finally satisfy them, and Dietrich Bonhoeffer has called up a cloud of witnesses whose fingers are pointed to the verse about keeping God's commandments.

I wade through the mob in my study to my bookcase and pull out *The Gospel According to John, XIII-XXI* by Raymond E. Brown. Nobody leaves, but everybody quiets down.

"According to John."

I have never before been so struck by that phrase, "According to." There are so many other ways the Gospel might have been titled: "The One and Only True Account of Jesus" or "Exclusive Inside Story" or "Lone Witness to Jesus" or simply "The Gospel Truth." But, no, that is not what we read. It is the Gospel *According to* John, not According to Matthew or According to Luke or According to Mark, but According to John, according to the way John saw things and according to the way he experienced and expressed the truth. I am so impressed with this insight that I announce it to everybody in the room: "Look, this is John's slant on things. Do you see that in the title, *The Gospel According to John?* If the early church qualified even its most reliable witnesses to the truth, then maybe all of us can relax a little about pushing our own perspective. Whatever we believe and say is true; it is *according to* us:

It is the gospel *according to* Isabel Moore.

The gospel *according to* Andrea Winston.

The gospel *according to* Tom Troeger.

It is not THE GOSPEL, but the gospel from one particular perspective. And the church has decided that we have so many gospels from so many perspectives floating around that we have got to have a few by which to judge all the others. John is one of those. When I read 'the Gospel According to John,' I lay aside the gospel according to Tom Troeger and I check out what John saw, because I often discover that he sees what I am blind to and corrects my vision where it is distorted."

When I finish this little speech, I find my study strangely still. It is not the hollowness of before, when I was wishing that the air would thicken with the Divine Presence. Rather, it is the hush of space that is surrounded by invisible witnesses who in good time will reappear to help me with my words.

I open my commentary to Raymond Brown's translation and place my RSV Bible next to it. I read the first two verses of John 14:15-26 out loud from the commentary.

> "If you love me
> and keep my commandments,

then at my request
the Father will give you another Paraclete
to be with you forever."[2]

Paraclete. The word drops against my ear drum and bounces back out. I never hear my people speaking about Paracletes. Is it really necessary to keep that Greek form of the word? I look at the RSV. "Counselor." Camp counselor? Legal counselor? Family counselor? Guidance counselor? Career counselor? Financial counselor? I try to imagine what the word might mean to Isabel Moore or Andrea Winston or any of the others who gathered around the desk and who will be in church on Sunday. I look up the scholar's note. It does not help with my immediate question. It focuses on the qualifier, "another," rather than on "Paraclete."

I pull out my Greek New Testament. I am not a great Greek scholar, but I am good enough to follow the text closely with the aid of those who are. I find the verse and read it in Greek, sneaking a couple of glances at the RSV to help me where I stumble. *Paraklaton.* There it is, "Paraclete" in Greek.

I look up the word in my Greek lexicon:

. . . "one who is called to someone's aid." Accordingly the Latin translators commonly rendered it, in its [New Testament] occurrences, with "advocatus". . . . But the technical [meaning] "lawyer," "attorney" is rare. . . . In the few places where the word is found in pre-Christian and extra-Christian [literature] it has for the most part a more general [meaning]: *one who appears in another's behalf, mediator, intercessor, helper.* . . . In our [literature] the [actual] sense *helper, intercessor* is suitable in all occurrences of the word. . . .[3]

Helper. Now that is a word people know. When they are drowning, they call, "Help!" When their friends see them through a crisis, they say, "You really helped me through" or "I don't know what I would have done without your help." I write these phrases down on my note pad. They are already touching off stories in me of people who have helped one another.

Then I look up how other translators have handled the word. Phillips' paraphrase is graphic: " . . . I shall ask the Father to give you Someone else to stand by you, to be with you always." That is what Isabel Moore is looking for: someone else to stand by her. She stood by her father all those years that he was lying in bed an invalid, and she did not realize that he was standing by her as much as she was by him. That is the way it is. The chronically ill make us as dependent on them as they are on us. Then one day they are gone, and we need someone to stand by us.

I copy down Phillips' paraphrase and write a four-line sermon outline:

"She stood by him for years."
He died: black holes in the ground, beyond the stars, at
    life's center.
Help!
"I shall ask the Father to give you Someone else to stand
    by you."

I return to Brown's translation and read the next verse (v. 17):

"He is the Spirit of Truth
whom the world cannot accept
since it neither sees nor recognizes him;
but you do recognize him
since he remains with you and is within you."

I turn to the commentary's note on the verse and discover that there is an entire appendix on "The Paraclete"! Reading a biblical text is just like listening to Peter Linden or Andrea Winston: there is so much more underneath the surface of the words than we first suspect.

For each must learn in each
all the dark-rooted language under speech. . . .[4]

That is what I am doing with this commentary on my desk. I am learning all the dark-rooted language under John's speech. Raymond Brown is digging up and untwisting

. . . the roots we did not know,
strong stems, dark stains, rich glories never guessed. . . .[5]

The richest glory of all comes at the very end of the appendix on "The Paraclete." The final sentence reads, "The Christian need not live with his eyes constantly straining toward the heavens from which the Son of Man is to come; for, as the Paraclete, Jesus is present within all believers."[6] I hear someone step back into the office and look over my shoulder.

"Read that again, that last sentence," says the elder of Unknown Spirit.

"The Christian need not live with his eyes constantly straining toward the heavens. . . ." I break off my reading and tell the elder, "You don't have to keep looking beyond the stars and the black holes, 'for, as the Paraclete, Jesus is present within all believers.'"

The elder does not say these next words, yet I can see them in his face: "'I believe; help my unbelief!' (Mark 9:24b). I believe in the Unknown Spirit. I know God has got to be in us, in me. But where? How?"

I go back to the beginning of the appendix and I go through the four meanings that Brown has listed for "Paraclete." And after each one I try to think of an experience that is common to contemporary life through which the elder may have had the slightest glimpse, the smallest taste, the gentlest touch of the reality behind the word.

Brown writes that if there is any legal meaning to the term, "the role of the Paraclete is that of a prosecuting attorney proving the world guilty."[7] When do we sense that the world is guilty? When do we feel judgment about the way the world lives? When we look at the evening news and see the boat people and the bombed and the starved, that is when the voice of judgment cries out.

SWOOSH!

SPIRIT!

That's it. The Paraclete is not beyond the stars and the black holes but is stirring inside us when we watch the evening news.

Next, Brown speaks of the Paraclete as "helper" or "inter-preter." Although he finds this language "too general to be of much value,"[8] I do not. I put the two meanings—"helper" and "interpreter"—together and remember a woman who once helped me through the slow death of a friend by interpreting the dying person's experience. Through her I felt a spirit of understanding that helped my friend and me to let go of each other.

SWOOSH!

SPIRIT!

That's it. The Paraclete is not an Unknown Spirit but the power of compassion that moves between people in profound pain.

The Paraclete is a "*consoler* of the disciples for he takes Jesus' place among them."[9] "A consoler, like your wife to you," I say to the elder of Unknown Spirit. "You know, the feeling that caresses your heart when you take her hand. At least that is a hint of the Paraclete, a clue to what it means."

Finally, the Paraclete is related to "the exhortation and en-couragement found in the preaching of the apostolic witness-es."[10] I remind the elder of the circle of eighteen elders and the open sharing of our images of God and the words of support and encouragement we gave one another.

SWOOSH!

SPIRIT!

That's it. The Paraclete is known in a conversation about the deepest meanings of life and faith.

Again and again the great wild red falcon is swooping down from heaven and swimming up from the depths as I struggle with the text. I write down another brief sermon outline:

Stars. Savior in the heavens. Millennium now? No.

"The Christian need not live with his [or her] eyes constantly straining toward the heavens from which the Son of Man is to come; for, as the Paraclete, Jesus is present within all believers." Really? How?

Judge—TV news.
Interpreter—friend's death.
Consoler—wife, husband, friend.
Encouragement—18 elders.

I turn back to Raymond Brown's translation in the commentary and read verse 18:

> "I shall not leave you orphans:
> I am coming back to you."

The letter *o* in "orphans" loops around my neck and tugs me

closer to the text. Orphans? I do not recall any orphans in the
RSV. I read the verse out of my Bible: "I will not leave you
desolate; I will come to you." I pick up my Greek text and
discover the word in debate is *orphanos*. It sounds like the very
root from which we get our English word "orphan." I look it up
in the lexicon: *"orphaned*—1. [literally] = *deprived of one's parents."*[11] Isabel Moore! The translation makes all the difference
in the world. The difference between "I will not leave you
desolate" and "I shall not leave you orphans" is the difference
between prose and poetry, generalized truth and truth that
makes us wince, between saying something instructive and
grabbing the congregation where they live.

"I shall not leave you orphans." I will not leave you without
a parent. You won't be a motherless child. You won't be a
fatherless daughter.

I look up Brown's note on orphans: "This figure of speech is
not unusual: the disciples of the rabbis were said to be orphaned
at their death . . . , as were the disciples of Socrates at his death
(*Phaedo* 116A)."[12] *Phaedo!* I remember reading it in college my
freshman year in Introduction to Philosophy. The course was
part of my journey away from faith, the good old freshman
rebellion routine, sanctifying adolescent needs with the facile
appropriation of great minds. I get out *Phaedo* and reread the
dialogue that recounts Socrates' last hours, the argument for the
immortality of the soul, and his final drinking of the poison:

> . . . Then raising the cup to his lips, quite readily and cheerfully
> he drank off the poison. And hitherto most of us had been able
> to control our sorrow; but now when we saw him drinking, and
> saw too that he had finished the draught, we could no longer
> forbear, and in spite of myself my own tears were flowing fast; so
> that I covered my face and wept, not for him, but at the thought
> of my own calamity in having to part from such a friend.[13]

I put the book down on the desk, opened to this final scene.
The letter *o* loops around my neck again and pulls me back to
the gospel: "I shall not leave you orphans:/I am coming back to
you."

"Someone is tapping on thick stone." Something is tapping
on my imagination. It is the beak of the wild red falcon. The
Spirit is trying to get into my mind. Tap, tap, tap. Knock, knock,
knock. Something is cracking open inside of me, an insight, a
memory, a scene of Jesus' disciples that captures their grief at
his loss. I pull a book out of my bookcase and thumb through
the closing chapters. Here's the scene I want. The sabbath after
the crucifixion of Jesus was beginning. Nine of the disciples

. . . sat gloomily gnawing their knuckles or bits of bread, worrying about the absent Little James and John, mostly hating the very smell of themselves. Thaddeus absently played a tune on his flute. Matthew growled:

"Will you please *stop*?"

"Sorry," said Thaddeus, flicking the spit from the instrument. "It was the piece I played for the girl's funeral when he—you know. It isn't forbidden, by the way, to play the flute on the Sabbath. Playing is not working."

"The question is," said Matthew, "what do we do?"

"One day at a time," said Bartholomew. "We do nothing till after the Sabbath."

"He means," the first James said, "what do we do if it's not, you know, true? If he doesn't—"

"He will, he will," growled Peter. "Have you all forgotten how to believe?"

"We all ought to have gone," Simon said. "Not just left it to John and Little James. I'm surprised at the other James here. I thought you would have been—well, the two Jameses were almost one James. It didn't mean much, did it, when it came to—doing something, well, serious—"

"I was sick," said James sullenly. "You saw me. Everything came up. Knot in my belly. Damn, you saw me. I could hardly move."

"They should be back by now," said Thomas. "For all we know they might have—"

"We would have heard," said Peter. "Even here. One of the women, perhaps—"

"The women didn't hide, did they?" said Philip. "The women stayed."

"Ah, make a song of it," said Matthew harshly. "Our big word was *prudence*. Keeping the message safe. There's always an excuse for cowardice. But cowardice it is and was. I'm going into town now. Who'll come?"

"No journeys on the Sabbath," said Thaddeus.

"We never worried about that before," Andrew said.

"It's right enough, though," said Matthew. "Picked up by one of the guardians of the faith. Taken in for—something or other."

"He's buried now," Peter said. "He's bound to be buried. Somewhere. God knows where."

Andrew cleared his throat and said: "We behaved badly."

Peter howled: "*I* behaved—God help me, God forgive me—"

"Oh, enough of that," snapped Thomas. "We've all had enough of that."

"We all behaved badly," Bartholomew said. . . .[14]

When you get down to their basic humanity, there is no difference at all between Socrates' weeping students and Jesus' disciples, grief-stricken and grumbling at one another. No difference at all except for this promise, "I shall not leave you orphans: I am coming back to you." No difference at all except for the Spirit.

SWOOSH!

SPIRIT!

I write down another sermon outline:

Scene 1:   The death of Socrates.
Scene 2:   The death of Jesus.
Transition: No difference at all. Tears are tears.
No difference EXCEPT THE PROMISE OF THE SPIRIT.
Scene 3:   "When the day of Pentecost had come. . . ."
    Litany—do with the choir.
Scene 4:   Pentecost now. Four stories from the outline on
    meaning of "Paraclete."
End with choice—T. S. Eliot lines.

It's coming. It's coming. The sermon. Can you see it? Not just the outline but the sermon. Socrates is in his cell lifting up the cup of hemlock. Can you hear it? Thaddeus is playing his flute. Can you taste it? The disciples are "gnawing their knuckles or bits of bread." Can you feel it inside you? Wind is howling and fire is raging and you've got to decide.

> The only hope, or else despair
>   Lies in the choice of pyre or pyre—
>   To be redeemed from fire by fire.

And the wind is howling and the fire is raging inside me as

I return to the biblical text, so that I tend to read straight through verse nineteen without fully comprehending the words. The letters register on my retinas, but the sense never makes it to my brain:

> "In just a little while the world will not see me any more;
> but you will see me
> because I have life and you will have life."

But then the next verse stops me cold again:

> "On that day you will recognize
> that I am in the Father,
> and you are in me, and I in you."

It is the word "recognize" that captures my attention. "Recognize." That is what Andrea Winston needs to do. "She's a beauty and she doesn't see it." Her husband wants her to recognize herself for who she is. "Recognize." I write the word down on my pad and then turn to the Greek text, eager to see if there is something special behind Raymond Brown's rendering. The word in Greek is *ginosko,* and I can understand from the lexicon why the RSV chose the plainer English word "know." Still, I cannot get the word "recognize" out of my system, and I again look at my parallel English translations. Most favor "know," but Phillips paraphrases, "When that day comes, you will *realise* that I am in my Father, that you are in me, and I am in you" (emphasis added). I like the word "realize" even better than "recognize." I think of all the common uses of the word: "Didn't you realize to whom you were talking?" "I suddenly realized what was happening." "I never realized it until it was too late."

All of a sudden an image of Andrea Winston forms in my mind. She is now in her eighties and her husband is dying, and there is great sadness on his face, sadness deeper than the sadness in the eyes of Andrea's self-statue. She is by his bed and he is asking her to bring a mirror from the bureau and she does. He says, "Look. See the beauty I have always seen." She looks in the mirror. A look flashes back at her from the bottom of her own heart that says, "I am beautiful because in my husband's eyes I am beautiful." This all happens in the time it takes light to travel from the mirror to her face. Then Andrea looks at her husband, her eyes shining with their natural beauty. For the first time in their marriage she realizes that she is a beauty—and then she realizes her husband is dead.

It is all a fantasy, but an important fantasy because it is drawing the fire of the spirit into my bones and making me burn with eagerness to help Andrea realize that she is in Christ and Christ is in her.

> "Whoever keeps the commandments that he has from me
> is the man who loves me;
> and the man who loves me will be loved by my Father,
> and I shall love him
> and reveal myself to him."

"The mention of indwelling in 20 is followed in 21 [above] by the condition on which that indwelling depends: keeping Jesus' commandments and thus loving him."[15] Again the air thickens with a cloud, and I see Bonhoeffer through the eyes of the physician who witnessed his death: "In the almost fifty years that I worked as a doctor, I have hardly ever seen a man die so entirely submissive to the will of God." I find myself speaking to Dietrich as if I were a monk praying to a saint: "O Brother Dietrich, is this what you knew at the gallows—that whoever keeps the commandments of Christ shall see Christ?"

Yes.

I actually hear the word. It sounds again and again. Yes, yes! YES! Like a crescendo that leads back into the hymn "For All the Saints":

> O may Thy soldiers, faithful, true, and bold,
> Fight as the saints who nobly fought of old,
> And win with them the victor's crown of gold . . .!

Then stillness. Long stillness.

My eyes finally drift back to the commentary (v. 22):

> "Lord," said Judas (not Judas Iscariot), "what can have happened
> that you are going to reveal yourself to us and not to the world?"

I am not thinking as clearly as I ought to right now. I will probably miss something in the text. I read the commentary and I look at the Greek, but my study is mechanical. I am still blazing with my earlier insights. It is hard to come back to the letter of the passage when the Spirit has taken over. I find myself chuckling at the way Jesus' questioner is identified: "Judas (not Judas Iscariot)." People are always eager to make sure the finger does not point at them. I read Brown's conclusion that because of the "confused evidence, no decision is possible" about who this Judas really was.[16] Then I formulate in my brain a speculative scene. John the Evangelist is with his school of disciples and he is reading the first draft of his Gospel after the fashion of the Muratorian Fragment that claims that John related "all things in his own name, aided by the *revision* of all."[17] John reads this passage from his draft: "'Lord,' said Judas, 'what can have happened . . .?'" "Hey, wait a minute," calls out one of the listeners named Judas. "You don't just use the name 'Judas.' You gotta make it clear which Judas. All of us ain't rotten apples just because the one was. Put in the words 'not Judas Iscariot.'" John does, and there it is in the text in parentheses. And I suppose that all the Judases (not Judas Iscariots) that have ever lived since then have been glad for the addition because they know the guilt has been placed on the right person (not them).

SWOOSH!

SPIRIT!

An idea for another sermon arises out of my fantasy: the issue is not simply innocence but obedience. "Okay, so you're not Judas Iscariot; you're Judas Jones. We know you didn't do anything evil. And God knows that. But did you do anything good? Did you feed someone who was hungry or forgive someone?"

> "If anyone loves me,
> he will keep my word.
> Then my Father will love him,
> and we shall come to him
> and make our dwelling place with him.
> Whoever does not love me does not keep my words;
> yet the word that you hear is not my own
> but comes from the Father who sent me."
> —John 14:23-24

People have a hard enough time keeping their own words. How can they be counted on to keep Christ's word? Couples promise they will be faithful and loving partners "for better, for worse, for richer, for poorer, in sickness and in health as long as we both shall live." Then the bills accumulate and the transmission falls out of the car, and one person grows sour and the other grows silent. Companies promise: "We unconditionally guarantee this product to be utterly free from all defects in material and workmanship for one year." So you turn the thing on and the switch falls off, and you take it back to the store and what do they say? The contractor signs on the dotted line that the floor in the bedroom will be refinished by June 15, and on June 16 you are still sleeping out on the porch. But here is Christ telling us that "If anyone loves me, he will keep my word." Which word? It is not perfectly clear from the text, especially since the following verse pluralizes the word, "Whoever does not love me does not keep my words," and then goes back to the singular, "yet the word that you hear is not my own but comes from the Father who sent me." It is very confusing to me. But Raymond Brown explains why the "variation between singular and plural in the use both of 'word' and 'commandment' (NOTE on 15) is not of clear theological significance."[18] Wait. What is this "NOTE on 15"? I go back and reread the note on verse 15. I had gotten so carried away with understanding "Paraclete" that I skipped over the comments on the opening verse, "If you love me and keep my commandments. . . ." "His commandments are not simply moral precepts: they involve a whole way of life in loving union with him."[19] Brown's note recalls a conversation I had with a young man who was hitchhiking across the country. "I don't want to be tied down. I just want to follow the breeze." All the hitchhiker wanted was spirit, not law. But it is clear that for John the two are not opposites. My eye selectively scans the text and lifts out a single thread that weaves in and out of all the words: "If you love me/and keep my commandments,/then . . ./the Father will give you another Paraclete/. . . . Whoever keeps the commandments that he has from me/is the man who loves me;/. . . . If anyone loves me,/he will keep my word./. . . Whoever does not love me does not keep my words." The text is as filled with law as with Spirit! But I did not see it until this moment. I had come with my eyes set only to see Spirit because it was Pentecost and because I had just finished reading Acts 2. But now I see that word and Spirit, commandment and grace, law and love are of one piece in John.

SWOOSH!

SPIRIT!

I write down another brief sermon outline:

Title: "Follow the Breeze"
A parable about the philosophy of our times: hitchhiker story.
Good for hitchhiking.
Not so good for marriages, products, and contracts.
How do we wind the wind into our marriages, friendships, businesses?
"If you love me/and keep my commandments,/then at my request/the Father will give you another Paraclete/to be with you forever."

All the dark-rooted language under speech is spaded over and exposed on the top of my desk. Socrates is drinking the hemlock next to Thaddeus playing his flute. John's Greek text lies parallel to Raymond Brown's English one. My notes about Isabel Moore and the elder of the Unknown Spirit are scribbled on the same pad of paper with my outlines. And the great wild red falcon is beating its wings over the face of all this as I leave the room to get a cup of coffee, whistling "The Heavens Are Telling the Joy of Thy Creation."

Rich Glories Never Guessed

"What shall I preach about on Sunday?"

How distant that question seems from me at this moment, almost as if it were in a foreign language. That is not how I would put the matter now. The question centers too much on me, "What shall *I* preach about on Sunday?" as though I were the only one involved in formulating the message. What about John the Evangelist and Raymond Brown and T. S. Eliot and all those parishioners who gathered around my desk and Bauer, Arndt, and Gingrich who put together that massive Greek lexicon and the members of the Lutheran Church–Missouri Synod whose Centennial Thank-offering helped pay for its publication and the printers who typeset it and must have gone blind getting all those foreign phrases down accurately and Dietrich Bonhoeffer and the cloud of witnesses he brought into my office and the great wild red bird of the Holy Spirit—what about all of these who are working on Sunday's sermon with me?

And the verb phrase in the question, "preach about," that is wrong too. It sounds as if I will speak about some topic in the same way the president speaks about the economy or a teacher lectures about history. My studies have not been teaching me *about* the Spirit. They have been leading me *into* the Spirit and the Spirit into me. It has been more exploration than explanation.

Finally, the question relates the sermon to only one point in time—"on Sunday." But in my study I have been related to an entire history stretching from the death of Socrates through the story of Jesus and Pentecost to the members of my congregation.

"What shall I preach about on Sunday?" The question is all wrong. It implies that preaching is the act of a solitary self speaking on an isolated topic at a singular point in time. There is no hint of the community's participation in the sermon, no recognition that the word that needs to be spoken may already be circulating in the listeners' lives.

The preaching of the early church was never such an isolated act. It depended on oral tradition, bits and pieces of stories and traditions that were passed along by the community. Neither the Gospel According to Matthew nor the Gospel According to Mark nor the Gospel According to Luke nor the Gospel According to John was the creation of a solitary self speaking on an isolated topic at a singular point in time. Remember my fantasy about Judas (not Judas Iscariot)? That was fiction, but it was based on a tradition that John related "all things in his

own name, aided by the *revision* of all." Imagine John's community listening to the evangelist's final draft or to the manuscript that some secretary wrote down, which might have been
the case with John.

"In the beginning was the Word, and the Word was with
God, and the Word was God," reads the evangelist.

"What a fine idea, to open with one of our favorite hymns!"
whispers someone in the circle. Then another listener breaks
into song, and by verse 3 everybody is singing.

The evangelist puts down the manuscript and looks a little
disgusted. "Do you want to hear this thing or not?" The voices
trail off and people are silent again. "And the Word became
flesh and dwelt among us, full of grace and truth." Tears roll
down the face of Lysander, a recent disciple. He does not know
the hymn yet, and the idea of the Word becoming flesh, becoming a slave like himself who has athlete's foot from scrubbing
the master's baths stirs him deeply. The evangelist hears him
sniffing and pauses while the slave wipes his nose with his
sleeve.

Then there is deep silence until the wedding at Cana. Cleopas
the Wino begins to chuckle and Stephen pokes him in the ribs
and whispers, "That's not what the story is about," and Cleopas
sobers up for the moment.

Then all we hear is the voice of the evangelist for several
chapters, except for now and then when people stop to nod
their heads or to look at the person who had contributed a
certain detail about which his mother or father or great-aunt had
told him.

When the evangelist gets into chapter 5 and Jesus is asking
the man at the pool of Bethesda, "Do you want to be healed?"
Sylvia, who is sitting on the floor between her crutches, calls
out, "Yes, Lord. Oh, I want to be healed." And the evangelist
stops and everyone looks at her, and in the silence you can hear
them praying what they have been praying for years over her:
"Lord, heal Sylvia, heal Sylvia." And although she does not get
up and walk, you would think she was healed from the way
her face shines when the evangelist reads, "And at once the
man was healed, and he took up his pallet and walked." Bar-
nabas puts his hand on Sylvia's shoulder and she holds on to
it and the story continues.

When they get to the story of feeding the five thousand, one
of them tiptoes back to the table and gets the bread that is left

from supper and pours some wine and passes it around. And everyone tears off a hunk of bread and takes a sip of wine, only Cleopas the Wino finishes the cup of wine off before it has gotten all the way around so that someone has to go back and fill it again.

Then the circle grows silent again until the healing of the blind man, when everyone looks at Neuronius because his father had been healed by a man who had been converted by one of the apostles. At least that is what Neuronius claims, though some doubt it because Neuronius is always changing the name of the apostle when he tells the story.

When they get to the raising of Lazarus, the place is as still as the tomb in Bethany where they laid him. "I am the resurrection and the life," reads the evangelist, and Claudius, who has just lost his wife, squeezes his daughter's hand. "Jesus wept."

"He wept?" asks Lysander, the recently converted slave, in a whisper. He has a lot of stories and hymns yet to learn. Stephen whispers back to him, "Yeah, his eyelids was puffy from crying. That's what I heard. He had all the power, power enough to raise a man from death, and he wept. Something, ain't it?"

The evangelist asks for them to pass the wine so that he can wet his whistle, and while he drinks, people mutter their first critical reactions: "It's okay, John." "You got it down straight this time." Then John clears his throat, and after instructing them, "Save me some of that bread for when I'm finished," he continues. When he gets to the washing, James, who is standing next to Lysander, puts his arm around the slave. This is the story that converted Lysander. Even now the slave is shaking his head in astonishment and whispering, "A Lord who'd wash his servant's feet." And Lysander tries to imagine his owner washing his feet, but he cannot picture it because it would never be.

Then the evangelist suggests they move back to the dinner table and sit down for the Last Discourse; and they do, though the dishes have not been cleared away and the air is stale with food hardening on plates.

"Let not your hearts be troubled; believe in God, believe also in me." The evangelist's voice is strong and calm now, even after so much reading. No one stirs. They want to hear every word from their Lord. "Judas (not Iscariot)——" The evangelist pauses and looks down the table to Judas, who winks his approval.

When they get to the trial and Pilate's skepticism—"What is truth?"—somebody quips, "That's a Roman for you!" People shush him quickly. They do not want any interruptions now. And there are no more until the evangelist reads, "So because of the Jewish day of Preparation, as the tomb was close at hand, they laid Jesus there." The evangelist puts down the manuscript for a minute and asks for a little more wine while people readjust themselves in their seats. But none of them speak. They are waiting in stone-still silence for the words that make all the other words more than the telling of a tragic tale.

The evangelist picks up the manuscript and resumes reading. "Now on the first day of the week Mary Magdalene. . . ."

When Thomas declares he has to see the holes in the body before he believes, Lysander shakes his head. He had agreed with Thomas when he first heard the story. Jesus' rising from death was too good to be true. Then the slave had gotten hooked on that story about the foot washing and he had decided to come to a meal with his friend. He had heard these stories from the whole community and something stirred in him. It was like a voice saying "Come forth." And he did and he believed and he was baptized.

"But there are also many other things which Jesus did," reads the evangelist in a husky whisper. "Were every one of them to be written, I suppose that the world itself could not contain the books that would be written." John puts the manuscript down on the table and gets a grease spot on it. "I added that last note just so people would know we had more to tell than we got down here. I figure that if they like this much, they'll come to us seeking more." But there is no need for John to sound apologetic, because the entire community loves the story, the details, and the way he got it all down. They feel a part of the story because they helped in the telling of it.

John related "all things in his own name, aided by the *revision* of all." And come Sunday, we preachers will have to relate all things with our own voices and faces and gestures and words. But why not, like John, be "aided by the *revision* of all"? If not by all, then by some, by the ruling board of our church, perhaps. Most denominations charge the ruling boards with pastoral responsibility, and every Protestant church speaks of the priesthood of all believers. Yet these ideals are seldom realized. Corporate sermon preparation provides an opportunity to put these theological affirmations into action. Why not try an agenda like this?

AGENDA

Prayer
Sermon preparation
Approval of the minutes
Treasurer's report
Mission committee
Christian education
Property committee: decision on the furnace

I know people are going to want to talk all night about the furnace. Some are going to tell how they had theirs cleaned and fixed and it was sixteen hundred dollars less than a new one; and some are going to say that the reason people are not coming to church is that it is too cold in the sanctuary; and some are going to deliver a salvo against OPEC; and they are all going to come eager to get their lines in. Furnaces are important but so is the flame in the heart. Think of John's community of believers listening to the evangelist and recognizing how they fit into the story because they have had a part in putting the story together. Maybe that is why the early church was so vibrant. The preaching was not a solo but a symphony. The evangelist was the conductor, but everyone had a part to play.

Spirit!

"Hear now from the Gospel According to John as put together primarily by him but with important contributions, observations, comments, and corrections from Cleopas the Wino, Lysander with athlete's foot, the crippled Sylvia, Neuronius, whose father was healed by a man converted by an apostle, Claudius the widower, Judas (not Iscariot) and others." If we had enough detailed historical knowledge of the communities from which the New Testament sprang, that might be how we would announce the lessons on Sunday. It would be quite a mouthful to say. People would think we were finished with the lesson by the time we came to the end of the title, and in a way we would be finished with a lesson, a very important lesson: The gospel is not the property of the preacher but the community. And if the preacher preaches well, the sermon, too, will belong to the entire congregation. The members of the congregation will sense they are listening to "the gospel as put together primarily by the preacher but with important contributions, observations, comments, and corrections by Isabel Moore; Peter Linden; the lady of smooth-skinned, athletic Jesus; the elders of Intimate Being, Unknown Spirit, Personal Jesus, Tender Mother, Judging Father, Healing Savior, Loving Christ, Creator Spirit, and God the Vague; plus Andrea Winston and her husband; T. S. Eliot; Plato; Raymond Brown; Bauer, Arndt, and Gingrich; Dietrich Bonhoeffer; John the Evangelist 'and Company'; and the great wild red bird of the Holy Spirit."

I step into the pulpit. We all bow our heads in prayer. "May the words of my mouth and the meditations of all our hearts be acceptable in your sight, O God, our rock"—Peter Linden is in his bog—"and our redeemer. Amen."

A one-page outline for the entire sermon sits on the pulpit stand.[20] You will recognize where it came from because you were in the study with me. I have made some changes, but I have deliberately not written it out word-for-word because I want to leave room for the Spirit and because it is the community's sermon and we cannot be sharing if my head is buried in a manuscript. I have practiced preaching it several times while I played the Sanctus from Bach's *B-Minor Mass* in the background. The music helped put me in touch with the Spirit. This use of music is an ancient method for being filled with God's Word. You can read 1 Samuel 10:5 if you want to see it at work in the Bible.

I look out from the pulpit and see people I love.

"Philip wiggled his toes. His feet still smelled soapy from Jesus' having washed them, but his palms were sweaty.

"'Set your troubled hearts at rest,' said Jesus, his eyes scanning those around the table. 'Believe in God.' Philip looked down and studied a knothole next to his plate. 'Believe also in me.' Thomas drummed his fingers like a patron at a restaurant not happy with what is served and eager to leave. 'I go and prepare a place for you. You know the way there.'

"'Lord,' Thomas blurted out, 'We do not know where you are going. How can we know the way?'

"'I am the way.' Jesus said more than that, but Thomas was so anxious that he caught only the first four words, and they quickly drowned in an ocean of doubt.

"Philip looked up from the knothole next to his plate. 'Lord, show us the Father, and we shall be satisfied.' Everyone leaned forward. Philip was demanding what they all desired."

The different vocal inflections for the various characters may sound complex, as though I have had to spend hours practicing the drama of this sermon. But that is not the case. I have been listening to how people speak in my house, at parties, on the beach, in restaurants, in stores, on the radio and television. And I have discovered that people do not just have one voice. They have many voices. They have a voice they use when their child has walked into the house with muddy shoes and another voice when they order French fries and a hamburger and another voice when they are disagreeing about how to solve inflation and another voice when they are walking on the beach and another voice when the ladder is slipping away from the wall and another voice when they are in a hurry to get off the phone. I have found that I, too, have all of these voices inside of me and that inflections of surprise, sadness, love, skepticism, and faith can engage a congregation by helping them to identify their own feelings and responses. Using these inflections is not a matter of melodrama but simply getting in touch with the natural emotional texture of the scene or character. So when I shift in the pulpit from Thomas to Jesus or from skeptic to believer, I am doing nothing more than the lady on the bus who tells her friend a fabulous story and exclaims: "I say to him, 'Ya gotta be kiddin'!'" But then he pulls the picture out of his wallet and, sure enough, I believe him."

My eyes glance down to the outline. "Jesus sighed, the sigh of parents who think their children are past a certain stage only to discover they are not. 'Have I been with you so long, and yet you do not know me, Philip?' Philip looked back at the knothole, embarrassed. Jesus had struggled to lead him to faith, but he still wanted proof. 'He who has seen me has seen the Father.' Philip's right hand traced the circumference of the knothole over and over while doubt and faith chased each other around and around in his head. It would take something greater than words to stop Philip's anxious circles."

I pause each time Thomas, Philip, or Jesus speaks, to let the congregation fill in their own questions and to let them hear Christ addressing them now. Like John's community that helped the evangelist revise his Gospel, my silence invites members of the congregation to bring their own revisions, their own doubts, and their own faith to the Lord.

I had considered using for the sermon my fictional account of John reading the final draft of his Gospel to the community.

But I am saving that for another Sunday. I decided that I needed to explore the gift of the Spirit on Pentecost Sunday since that is the focus of the lessons and since that is the pressing pastoral need represented by the elders of God the Vague and Unknown Spirit and Isabel Moore and Andrea Winston.

"'If you love me, you will keep my commandments.' Someone was hungry at the far end of the table and Philip stopped his nervous gesture to pass the man some bread. 'God will give you another Counselor, to be with you for ever, even the Spirit of truth.' Philip grabbed the words out of the air as eagerly as the disciple had taken the bread from his hand."

I stop circling my right forefinger on the manuscript stand and pass an imaginary loaf of bread from the choir on my left to an imaginary disciple on my right. The gesture may be more significant than anything I say. People can actually see what happens when I abandon my self-preoccupation to serve another. I can think of many sermons that I have seen and heard in which a simple gesture stayed with me long after the words had evaporated. The gesture then brought back the words, and the Word of God sounded in me again. Gestures are as important to think about as words. As in the case of vocal inflections, it is not a matter of melodrama but of being in touch with the natural movements of the human body that would characterize a scene or a character. Keep it simple. Keep it spontaneous and the point will flow through your arms and hands and body even as your words flow.

Become aware of what your own characteristic gestures are. They can be overdone. The number of congregations who want their preachers to stop pushing their glasses up on their nose must be legion! But preachers also err in the other direction. I recall that when I first started preaching, I had a very high pulpit and I used to lean forward on it with my arms folded and my elbows resting on the manuscript stand, especially when I told stories. Another preacher saw me do this and told me it was sloppy pulpit etiquette, so I stopped. In a few weeks someone said to me, "How come you aren't talking to us, the way you used to?" "What do you mean?" "Leaning forward, like you do, on your arms. Whenever you did that, it was like you were talking straight to each of us." In another church or on special occasions the posture may have been inappropriate; but I went back to it for the most part, and, sure enough, people started telling me, "You're talking to us."

Right now I am leaning on the pulpit like Philip over his knothole. "'God will give you another Counselor.' Philip turned the words over in his mind and examined all the dark-rooted language under Jesus' speech. Counselor, counselor. The word snagged Philip's attention. It was an unusually rich term that could mean many things, as I discovered this week in my study.

"Sometimes 'counselor' refers to an attorney or prosecutor, the voice of judgment that cries out against injustice. You and I have heard that voice. I am watching the television news and some refugees are getting on a boat that is already swamped with people, and my heart is crushed with the way we human beings treat one another. I do not feel superior, as though I would never be part of such cruelty. Instead, I feel a need to act. I hear a voice saying to me what Edmund Burke said: 'All that is needed for evil to triumph is for enough good people to do nothing.'

"That voice of judgment belongs to the Counselor whom Jesus promised at the table that night. It's the Spirit for whom Philip was hungering!

"Sometimes 'counselor' means helper, interpreter, someone who stands by us and makes sense out of our suffering. You and I have known this comfort, each in our own way. I picture myself in a hospital room, over ten years ago, visiting a friend who is dying, and I do not understand everything that is happening between us, the shifts from anger to peace and peace to anger. But a nurse speaks to me and helps me comprehend how my friend is saying good-bye. Through that nurse the pain of my friend's end is interpreted and both of us are helped. We feel the Spirit of strength moving between us.

"That strength is the Counselor whom Jesus promised at the table that night. It's the Spirit for whom Philip was hungering!

"Sometimes 'counselor' means the Spirit of encouragement and support for our faith. It is what the elders of this church felt when they sat in a circle trying to figure out how we see God and ourselves. Although we each have different visions and many disagreements, we spoke at the retreat with warm, strong voices, trying to encourage one another in our faith. We shared our common struggle, and before we sat down to eat pizza, we belted out the Doxology with gusto.

"Moving among us was the Counselor whom Jesus promised at the table that night. It's the Spirit for whom Philip was hungering."

I take a long pause. People need time to finish with the memories that have been awakened. They are preaching the sermon now, and they will be preaching it at the door and during the coffee hour when they share the stories of the Spirit that were awakened within them. I have deliberately started with these small human examples because I know that the splendid ecstasy of the Pentecost scene in Acts 2 is too exalted an opening for the elders of God the Vague and Unknown Spirit and Isabel Moore and Andrea Winston. I am working toward Pentecost by first identifying touches of the Spirit that will open the skeptics to the grander motions of God. I have a colleague who quotes a favorite saying of a former teacher: "Avoid a premature appeal to mystery."[21] That is good advice for us preachers. We are supposed to help the light shine in our listeners, but we won't do that if we wallpaper all of our sermons with mystery. This does not mean we never speak of mystery. After all, "faith is the assurance of things hoped for, the conviction of things not seen" (Hebrews 11:1); but we do not facilitate that faith by immediately starting a sermon, "The Spirit is a mystery too deep to understand." If that is the opening sentence of a sermon, it should also be the last. It is the Jacob's ladder principle again: start with the rungs closest to earth. "Philip wiggled his toes." Send an angel up before you call one down.

"'I shall not leave you orphans.' Philip returned from his reverie about the meaning of 'counselor' to hear that Christ would not abandon the disciples as motherless children, fatherless sons and daughters. They would not be left to fend for themselves as the followers of other great teachers. When Socrates was about to die, Phaedo, one of his best friends, wrote, 'he was like a father of whom we were being bereaved, and we were about to pass the rest of our lives as orphans.'[22] That was Philip's fear, the fear of all human beings, born in the baby's bone and crying out from the cradle:

> Am I abandoned?
> Are we alone or is someone with us?
> Do we walk down the midnight street by ourselves or is the arm of eternity wrapped in love around our waist?
> Is it true that the wisest and most just and best of all people die to leave us orphans?
> Are we here as 'on a darkling plain. . . . Where ignorant armies clash by night'?[23]

Or. . . .

Or is there a Counselor, even the Spirit of truth, who is with us forever?"

The questions expand from cradle to street to battlefield. I am trying to broaden the solitary consciousness of the listeners step-by-step so that they will see the need for dimensions of the Spirit greater than the circumference of their private lives.

"'I shall not leave you orphans.' Philip and the other disciples would have to wait for the promise of the Spirit to come true. They would have to wait through the arrest in the garden.

"They would have to wait through the trial.

"They would have to wait through the slow death on a cross.

"They would have to wait through the burial.

"They would have to wait even beyond the appearances of the risen Christ.

"They would have to wait and wait.

"Even as you and I must wait sometimes."

The repeated verbal formula is used to build the suspense toward the coming of the Spirit. I am using the story of the disciples' waiting to help the elders of God the Vague and Unknown Spirit and Isabel Moore understand their own painful waiting.

"But 'when the day of Pentecost had come, they were all together in one place. And suddenly a sound came from heaven like the rush of a mighty wind, and it filled all the house where they were sitting.'"

Members of the choir now join in the sermon by responding in unison to the questions in the litany.

Is this the wind that in the beginning moved across the deeps?
Yes, this is the gust that parted oceans, land, and sky.
Is this the wind that God breathed into our nostrils?
Yes, this is the breath that filled our lungs at birth.
Is this the wind that drove apart the waters of the sea?
Yes, this is the gale that made the Hebrews free.
Is this the wind Ezekiel called to make the dry bones dance?
Yes, this is the breeze that rattled them to life.
Is this the wind that blows away the cobwebs of the soul?
Yes, this is the gust that bears away our sin and makes us soar with grace.

I developed this wind litany following the gift of the fire that had flashed upon me in my study. Now I continue with the Acts 2 scene.

"'And there appeared to them tongues as of fire, distributed and resting on each one of them. And they were all filled with the Holy Spirit and began to speak in other tongues, as the Spirit gave them utterance.'"

Is this the fire that Moses saw?
Yes, this is the flame that burned in the bush and called the slaves to freedom.
Is this the fire that led by night across the desert wastes?
Yes, this is the flame that showed the way to the promised land.
Is this the fire that burned in Jeremiah's bones?
Yes, this is the flame that made the prophet rage with justice.
Is this the fire Isaiah saw that blazed with holiness?
Yes, this is the flame that cleansed his lips and sent him to the people.
Is this the fire that shines within our own deep hearts?
Yes, this is the flame that burns within us with faith and hope and love.

After all of the human illustrations for "counselor" I want people to feel something of the majesty and mystery of God's Spirit from which we draw in our everyday lives. That is why I include the Pentecost scene and litany here. The vocal power of the choir's unison reading gives experiential texture to the words.

I had considered eliminating the Acts 2 scene altogether or putting the litany at another point in the service, because the theology of John and the theology of Acts are different. The John passage talks about the dwelling of the Spirit here and now, while Acts 2 is about a particular experience of the Spirit in the early church. I have overridden these considerations of biblical interpretation in light of what I consider to be the pressing pastoral need: the need to fuse together in my listeners the connections between the sublimity of the Spirit known on Pentecost and their daily experience. Another preacher might see it differently, and another congregation might require a different sermon altogether.

I have scrapped the Anthony Burgess scene of Thaddeus and the other disciples grumbling at one another. I had to. It did not fit. It took place between the burial and the resurrection, but Pentecost Sunday comes after the resurrection. So there was no way I could use it without making my chronology too complex. Besides, I want to focus on Pentecost. The gift of the Spirit is a large enough topic for one sermon. We do not have to cram everything into every sermon. That makes the gospel too full. It is too full for our listeners to absorb. We have the whole year. I will be using that scene from Burgess with the distraught disciples chewing their knuckles on some Good Friday or as the opening to a sunrise service. It is in my mind and in my files. But in this sermon I focus on the Spirit.

"Philip had traced the knothole around and around, and doubt and faith had circled inside him, even as they chase each other inside you and me. But Jesus stopped Philip's nervous circlings with the promise of the Spirit: 'If someone loves me, that person will keep my word, and my Father will love that person, and we will come to that person and make our home with that person.' Imagine: God at home inside of you. There is no greater compliment than someone saying to us, 'You made me right at home here.' It takes more than words to accomplish that. We have all visited someone who *says*, 'Make yourself right at home' but then fusses and fidgets so that we feel we are in a strange land. But we have also been to other places where our host relaxed and every action made us feel welcome, wanted, at home. It is the same with Christ. To make Christ at home in us requires not talk but action. 'If someone loves me, that person will keep my word, and my Father will love that person, and we will come to that person and make our home with that person.' If you love someone who hates you, you will be acting the way Christ acts and Christ will be at home in you. If you forgive someone who wrongs you, you will be acting the way Christ acts and Christ will be at home inside you. If you feed the hungry, if you take a stand for justice, you will be acting the way Christ acts and Christ will be at home in you. And through you Christ will be at home in the world.

"Sometimes when we take a vacation in a beautiful scenic area, we say, 'It's God's country.' But what the gospel tells us is that when we obey Christ, WE are God's country. We are God's home. We are where God lives. The beauty of heaven shines in us. When we keep Christ's commandments, we are filled with the Spirit as surely as the disciples were filled with the Spirit on the day of Pentecost.

"Who is at home inside you and me?

"To whom do we open our hearts?

"I once knew a woman who had room in her heart only for bitterness. Although her husband bequeathed her a fortune, she hated him because he had died young and left her with two children to raise on her own. She hated her children because they reminded her of her husband. She hated the nursing home where she moved at age eighty-seven, because everybody around her was old and she hated old people. I used to look at her eyes and they reminded me of old white china that has lost its glaze and turned gray and grainy. The inside of that woman was not God's country. It was a burned-out forest, a place where trees could have grown if so much bitterness had not raged there.

"What about you?

"What about me?

"Are we God's country?

"Or are we like that woman with the gray, grainy eyes?

"We have to decide what we are going to burn in life.

> The only hope, or else despair
> Lies in the choice of pyre or pyre—
> To be redeemed from fire by fire.

T. S. Eliot says our choice is 'pyre or pyre.' It is easy to stack all of our griefs and grudges in the middle of the soul and have a bonfire of bitterness. Bitterness is cheap fuel. It is easy to find plenty to burn. But if that is all we burn, we pretty soon will be burned-out.

"Who is at home in you and in me?

"Philip and the other disciples opened their hearts to Christ by obeying him. The Spirit came. The fire of faith redeemed them from the fire of doubt. The fire of love redeemed them from the fire of fear. Christ was at home inside them and among them.

"And if we keep Christ's commandments, he will be at home inside us and among us. The wisest and most just and best of all people is not dead. Christ is waiting for us even more expectantly than we are waiting for him. Christ is waiting to make his home inside of us. Christ is waiting for me, for you, for this church, for our bruised and bleeding world. Look up from your nervous circlings and listen again to the words that pulled Philip away from his doubt toward hope: 'If you love me, you will keep my commandments. And I will pray the Father, and he will give you another Counselor, to be with you for ever.'

"Listen.

"Obey.

"The Spirit will come."

I pause. I look over the congregation, and a dozen prayers

flash through my mind too fast and too private for me to utter aloud: "God, heal Isabel's grief. Help Peter grow up to find the rock. Keep the elder of Intimate Being open to those who believe less fervently. Do not let the elder of Personal Jesus overwhelm the others with his piety. Leap from beyond the stars and the black holes into the heart of the elder of the Unknown Spirit. Show the lady of smooth-skinned, athletic Jesus how Christ is in her suffering neighbor. Open Andrea Winston's inner eyes before it is too late. Amen." By the time I get to the end of this flood of silent petitions, I say out loud, "Let us pray. Holy Spirit, Sacred Flame, Rushing Wind, ..." I hear the beating of wings. ". . . redeem us from the fire of doubt by the fire of faith."

Some preachers do not believe that you should pray what you preach. In general they are right. It is a sound way to avoid preaching in our prayers. However, at the end of a sermon I often pray a brief prayer picking up on my imagery or phrases in hope that where words have faltered God's Spirit will take over.

"Redeem us from the fire of fear with the fire of love. Make your home with us and in us." The wings sound closer and closer, louder and louder. I look up. Most heads are bowed except for Peter Linden who is looking at the ceiling. I wonder if he sees it too. Red! "Make your home among us as we keep Christ's word in your world. Amen."

I look up. The great wild bird descends.

SWOOSH!

SPIRIT!

5

Postlude: A Whimsical Revelation of a Profound Truth

The organ is playing the postlude and people are shaking my hand at the door. The music is a gigue by Handel: Doodle doop, doodle doop, doodle doop doooo. Deedle deep, deedle deep, deedle deep deeee.

Peter Linden comes out and shakes my hand. "I'm wiggling my toes," he says, "like Philip."

I smile. Years ago I would have foolishly thought that the child did not get the point of the sermon. But the fact is, Peter did get the point. At least he got the point that is *his* point: namely, that there are in the gospel human beings like himself— they wiggle their toes—who follow Jesus. That much knowledge can be the seed that will grow into faith.

"Keep wiggling those toes," I tell him, and he responds, "I am, to the music."

Deedle deep, deedle deep, deedle deep deeee.

Isabel shakes my hand and indicates that she heard the message about the orphans by patting the back of my right hand and nodding her head. I offer a silent prayer to the witnesses in my office: "Thank you, Raymond Brown and Bauer, Arndt, and Gingrich."

"I liked the T. S. Eliot," says the woman of smooth-skinned, athletic Jesus. "We read him in the modern poetry course down at the library. He's hard to understand, but I got those lines all right. The choice is, What will we burn?"

"That's the choice," I say, while others who are eager to get home shake hands quickly and formally. I used to wonder if I had gotten through to these people, but I gave that worry up a long time ago when I saw a man in the hospital who had been dragged to church for years by his wife. At least that is what it looked like. During the sermon he used to sit next to her with his arms folded and his eyes rolled to the left, as though he had been cornered by a bore at a party. When I visited the man in the hospital, he spoke to me for nearly an hour, quoting my sermons back and showing how he had interpreted them to make sense out of his life. Evidently "each must learn in each all the dark-rooted language" under silence as well as speech. So now as a string of people file past with a quick nod or handshake, I do not assume it means they were not listening. Indeed, I try to assume nothing, for who knows what "strong stems, dark stains, rich glories never guessed" lie behind their public faces?

"I'm with Philip and Thomas," says the elder of God the Vague. But he says it with a light voice and a wink, suggesting that although the sermon has not made him sure about God, it has made him less doctrinaire about his skepticism, and that is a considerable advance forward.

Doodle doop, doodle doop, doodle doop doooooooooooooooo!

Andrea Winston and her husband come out last. They had been waiting for the postlude to finish. "We love Handel," says Andrea, whose eyes are shining as merrily as the music to which she has just listened. And as the Winstons leave, I reflect how Handel's *Gigue* probably did more for Andrea's soul than my words. I am not discouraged by this. I am, instead, awed by the complexity of grace, by the multitudinous ways that God untangles the spider web soul. The Spirit gets through one way or another: sometimes through images like the wild red falcon, sometimes through words like the gospel promise "I shall not leave you orphans," sometimes through people like Jeremy Brown's aunt "who art in heaven," sometimes through music like Handel's *Gigue*, sometimes through human touch such as Peter Linden's hand on top of Aunt Almeda's knobby joints, sometimes through the poet's fearful language such as "the sweat of interior stones." The Spirit, implacable and unpredictable, descends, and that is why I must preach: not because my words are the only way to redemption, but because I cannot contain myself for the excitement of telling all of the different ways God comes.

I return to my study. My books and notes are strewn across the desk like the pieces of Moses' shattered tablets. There is great truth here, if only it can be assembled. I have tried to do that this last week, and by Tuesday I shall be back at the task again. For now I peruse once again the outline which I have written today:

Redeemed from Fire by Fire

Philip wiggled his toes.
"Set your troubled hearts at rest."

Thomas, at restaurant, anxious and doubting.

Philip: "Show us the Father." Knothole.

Jesus sighs—like parent.
"If you love me, . . . keep commandments."
Philip passes bread.

Another Counselor: —Prosecutor: TV.
—Interpreter: hospital.
—Encouragement: 18 elders.

Not orphans: basic fear in bone.   Baby.
Street.
Battlefield.

OR Counselor.

Disciples have to wait through arrest, trial, etc.

But "when the day of Pentecost had come . . ." (see litany).

+ + + + + + + +   + + + + + + + +   (This is my symbol for silence and shift in tone and delivery).

Philip HAD traced knothole, but stopped by Spirit.

Imagine: God *at home* in us.

Explore mng. of phrase.

God's country.

Explore mng. of phrase.

Who is at home in us?
Woman with gray and grainy eyes.

A decision:

The only hope, or else despair
Lies in the choice of pyre or pyre—
To be redeemed from fire by fire.

Our choice: Easy to stack grudges. What will we burn?

Listen.

Obey.

Prayer: Redeem from fire of doubt by fire of faith.

Make your home in us and among us.

I review what went well and what went poorly. The scene at the table had them, and the old woman with gray and grainy eyes seemed to strike a chord. But the end meandered a little. I packed in too much stuff. Making Christ at home and "God's country" were both graphic ideas, but I think one would have been enough, although I am not sure. People liked the choral reading. Several members mentioned it, but I felt it would have been better for the entire congregation to participate in the litany, maybe after the reading of the Acts 2 passage or as a special call to worship or following the sermon.

I scribble a few notes on my sheet: "Opening scene—good. Tighten and rework ending." I will never be able to use exactly this sermon again. For sermons are like manna: what is fresh when it is first delivered quickly turns foul (Exodus 16:20). Most of us preachers have tasted old sermons in our own mouths. We have gone to the barrel and pulled out a sermon that was the bread of life in another time and place. But the yeast of the Spirit and the ferment in the community that first made it rise and gave it flavor have evaporated, and all we end up serving the second time around is the stale crust of an idea that once had the firmly grained texture of truth. However, I do save the sermon outline along with the sketches for other sermons I did not preach. In the future I will look back through this material and it will touch off new ideas, the same way the wild red bird came back to me months later.

I file away my papers. I begin to pick up my books from the desk. Good-bye, Socrates. Good-bye, Raymond Brown. Good-bye, Bauer, Arndt, and Gingrich. Good-bye, you whole wonderful mob of witnesses that helped me with this sermon.

As I get the last book away and survey a relatively barren desk, I feel drained, utterly "pooped." The study seems as hollow as when I started. I sit down and put my head on the desk. I breathe gently and think no thoughts and no words.

Silence.

Emptiness.

Exhaustion.

My desk, like Jacob's rock, is a pillow for fitful sleep.

Something is placed on the carpet in my study—a ladder, extended down to earth from above. The rungs that I have struggled all week to put in place now appear before me without any effort on my part. Someone is climbing down. It is the same angel who came with the orange sword at Christmas, only this time instead of a sword there appears to be a telegram in the messenger's hand. The angel is singing: Doodle doop, doodle doop, doodle doop doooo. Deedle deep, deedle deep, deedle deep deeee.

When the angel steps off the bottom rung, the gigue stops. The angel unrolls the telegram and reads:

In the beginning: God.

In the middle: God.

In the end: God.

Then the angel starts back up the ladder singing the gigue again. I watch the angel ascend, and with every deedle deep and every doodle doop I feel lighter and more energetic. The angel stops just before disappearing out of sight and calls down, "And remember this: listen to your own sermons."

Words rush through me like wind and fire, words that I have spoken but have not heard until this minute: "WE are God's country. We are God's home. We are where God lives. The beauty of heaven shines in us." And as the words whirl around inside of me, the ladder lifts upward from the study floor.

Someone is tapping. Tap, tap, tap. Knock, knock, knock. It is at the study door. I hear the voice of the head usher.

"I have finished locking up and checking everything. I'll remember the woman with the gray and grainy eyes. I gotta watch that myself. Good-bye. Have a good week."

"Oh, you too," I say in a groggy voice that I try to make cheerful and awake.

I walk out to the church parking lot. Everyone is gone. I look down at the blacktop and see where a blade of grass has pushed its way up through the hard surface. I turn and walk home, singing happily, "Deedle deep, deedle deep, deedle deep deeee," and thinking to myself, *"Surely the LORD is in this place; and I"*—the preacher who announced this truth to everybody else—*"did not know it."* But I know it now, and I feel in my bones what Bonhoeffer at long last realized: "Whoever I am, thou knowest, O God, I am thine."

Notes

Chapter 1

[1] Bunyan Davie Napier, *Come Sweet Death: A Quintet from Genesis* (Philadelphia: United Church Press, imprint of Pilgrim Press, 1967), p. 90. Reprinted with permission from *Come Sweet Death: A Quintet from Genesis* by Bunyan Davie Napier. Copyright © 1967 United Church Press; copyright © 1981 The Pilgrim Press.

[2] *Ibid.*

[3] Wolfhart Pannenberg, "Religious Experience—A Contemporary Possibility?" in *The Twentieth-Century Pulpit,* ed. James W. Cox (Nashville: Abingdon Press, 1978), p. 162. Copyright © 1978 by Abingdon. Used by permission.

[4] Excerpts from George Herbert, "The Flower," in *The Meditative Poem,* ed. Louis Martz (New York: Doubleday & Company, Inc., 1963), as cited in *The Oxford Book of Christian Verse,* ed. Lord David Cecil (1940; reprint ed., New York: Oxford University Press, Inc., 1951), p. 150. Copyright © 1963 by Louis L. Martz. Reprinted by permission of Doubleday & Company, Inc.

Chapter 2

[1] Mary Gordon, *Final Payments* (New York: Random House, Inc., 1978), p. 292.

[2] James Dickey and Marvin Hayes, *God's Images* (Birmingham: Oxmoor House, Inc., 1977); for the reader's convenience it may be noted that this sentence is the first sentence of the book's foreword.

[3] Excerpts from Theodore Roszak, *Where the Wasteland Ends* (New York: Doubleday & Company, Inc., 1972), p. 139. Copyright © 1972 by Theodore Roszak. Reprinted by permission of Doubleday & Company, Inc.

[4] The idea for this chart is not original with me. I picked up the concept in a conversation with another pastor several years ago. This particular chart, however, is one that I made up. If you try this with your own church, you may want to change some of the words to meet your particular needs. But it is very important that you stick to single, simple words.

138   Creating Fresh Images for Preaching

5The Joint Committee on Worship, *The Worshipbook: Services* (Philadelphia: The Westminster Press, 1970), p. 90.

6Roszak, *op. cit.*, pp. 110-111.

7John Calvin, *On the Christian Faith*, ed. John T. McNeill (New York: Liberal Arts Press, Inc., imprint of the Bobbs-Merrill Co., Inc., © 1957), p. 119.

8*Ibid.*, p. 98.

9Charles Garside, *Zwingli and the Arts* (New Haven: Yale University Press, 1966), p. 1.

10Paul Theroux, *Picture Palace* (Boston: Houghton Mifflin Company, 1978), p. 352. Copyright © 1978 by Paul Theroux. Reprinted by permission of Houghton Mifflin Company.

11*Ibid.*

12T. S. Eliot, "Burnt Norton," in *The Complete Poems and Plays*, 1909-1950 (New York: Harcourt Brace Jovanovich, Inc., 1952), p. 121.

13Fred B. Craddock, *As One Without Authority* (Enid, Okla.: The Phillips University Press, 1971). The entire book has influenced my discussion here.

14Gerard Manley Hopkins, "The Starlight Night," in *The Oxford Book of Christian Verse*, ed. Lord David Cecil (1940; reprint ed., New York: Oxford University Press, Inc., 1951), p. 495.

15Harold A. Carter, *The Prayer Tradition of Black People* (Valley Forge: Judson Press, 1976), p. 42.

16Craddock, *op. cit.*, p. 80.

17Annie Dillard, *Holy the Firm* (New York: Harper and Row, Publishers, Inc., 1977), p. 25.

18Reynolds Price, *A Palpable God* (New York: Atheneum Publishers, 1978), p. 53. Copyright © 1978 by Reynolds Price. Reprinted with the permission of Atheneum Publishers.

19*Ibid.*

20*Ibid.*, p. 54.

21Joseph G. Donders, *Jesus, the Stranger* (Maryknoll, N.Y.: Orbis Books, 1978), p. 18.

22*Ibid.*

23*Ibid.*, pp. 20-21.

24*Ibid.*, p. 21.

25Anthony Burgess, *Man of Nazareth* (New York: McGraw-Hill, Inc., 1979), pp. 33-34. Used with the permission of McGraw-Hill Book Company.

Chapter 3

1Gerhard von Rad, *Genesis, a Commentary*, trans. John H. Marks (Philadelphia: The Westminster Press, 1961), p. 58.

2Paul Theroux, *Picture Palace* (Boston: Houghton Mifflin Company, 1978), p. 96. Copyright © 1978 by Paul Theroux. Reprinted by permission of Houghton Mifflin Company.

3John Calvin, *On the Christian Faith*, ed. John T. McNeill (New York: Liberal Arts Press, Inc., imprint of the Bobbs-Merrill Co., Inc., © 1957), p. 3.

[4] Reinhold Niebuhr, *The Nature and Destiny of Man: A Christian Interpretation* (New York: Charles Scribner's Sons, 1947), p. 122.

[5] Calvin, *op. cit.*, emphasis added.

[6] Mary Gordon, *Final Payments* (New York: Random House, Inc., 1978), p. 57.

[7] Joseph G. Donders, *Jesus, the Stranger* (Maryknoll, N.Y.: Orbis Books, 1978), p. 20.

[8] Niebuhr, *op. cit.*

[9] Flannery O'Connor, *The Habit of Being,* ed. Sally Fitzgerald (New York: Farrar, Straus and Giroux, Inc., 1979), p. 594.

[10] This was a favorite story of an artist friend of mine; I do not know how precise the words are.

[11] O'Connor, *op. cit.*, p. 337.

[12] W. A. Visser 't Hooft, *Rembrandt and the Gospel,* trans. K. Gregor Smith (Philadelphia: The Westminster Press, 1957). The entire book has influenced my discussion here.

[13] James Dickey and Marvin Hayes, *God's Images* (Birmingham: Oxmoor House, Inc., 1977); for the reader's convenience it may be noted that this passage appears opposite plate 40 in the book. Reprinted with permission of the publisher, Oxmoor House, Inc.

[14] von Rad., *op. cit.*, p. 56.

[15] Bunyan Davie Napier, *Come Sweet Death: A Quintet from Genesis* (Philadelphia: United Church Press, imprint of Pilgrim Press, 1967), p. 90. Reprinted with permission from *Come Sweet Death: A Quintet from Genesis* by Bunyan Davie Napier. Copyright © 1967 United Church Press; copyright © 1981 The Pilgrim Press.

[16] T. S. Eliot, "Burnt Norton," in *The Complete Poems and Plays, 1909-1950* (New York: Harcourt Brace Jovanovich, Inc., 1952), p. 117.

[17] Dietrich Bonhoeffer, *Letters and Papers from Prison,* enl. ed. (New York: Macmillan Publishing Co., 1972), pp. 164-165. Reprinted with permission of Macmillan Publishing Co., Inc. Copyright © 1953, 1967, 1971 by SCM Press Ltd.

[18] O'Connor, *op. cit.*, p. 90.

[19] Gordon, *op. cit.*, p. 262.

[20] O'Connor, *op. cit.*

[21] Wallace Stevens, "Sunday Morning," in *The Collected Poems of Wallace Stevens* (New York: Alfred A. Knopf, Inc., 1965), pp. 66-67.

[22] *Ibid.*

[23] O'Connor, *op. cit.*

[24] *Ibid.*

[25] Eliot, *op. cit.*

[26] *Ibid.*

[27] Eberhard Bethge, *Dietrich Bonhoeffer,* trans. Eric Mosbacher *et al.,* and ed. Eric Robertson (New York: Harper and Row, Publishers, Inc., 1970), pp. 25-26. Original German edition Copyright © 1967 Chr. Verlag Munchen. English translation Copyright © 1970 William Collins Sons & Co., Ltd., London, and Harper & Row, Publishers, Inc., New York. Reprinted by permission of Harper & Row, Publishers, Inc.

[28] William Wordsworth, "'My Heart Leaps Up when I Behold,'" in

The Complete Poetical Works of Wordsworth, ed. Andrew J. George (Boston: Houghton Mifflin Company, 1932), p. 277.

[29] Carter Heyward, "Priesthood," in *Women and the Word: Sermons,* ed. Helen Gray Crotwell (Philadelphia: Fortress Press, 1978), p. 77.

[30] Carter Heyward, *A Priest Forever* (New York: Harper and Row, Publishers, Inc., 1976), pp. 6-7.

[31] Bonhoeffer, *op. cit.*, p. 164.

[32] *Ibid.*, p. 165.

[33] Eliot, *op. cit.*, p. 122.

[34] Bethge, *op. cit.*, pp. 830-831.

[35] Susan Sontag, *On Photography* (New York: Farrar, Straus and Giroux, Inc., 1977), p. 20.

[36] My former colleague, Richard Manzelmann, taught me this clever trick.

Chapter 4

[1] T. S. Eliot, "Little Gidding," in *The Complete Poems and Plays, 1909-1950* (New York: Harcourt Brace Jovanovich, Inc., 1952), p. 144.

[2] Raymond E. Brown, trans., *The Gospel According to John (xiii-xxi),* The Anchor Bible Series (New York: Doubleday & Company, Inc., 1970), vol. 29A, p. 637. Copyright © 1970 by Doubleday & Company, Inc. Reprinted by permission of the publisher.

[3] Walter Bauer, *A Greek-English Lexicon of the New Testament and Other Early Christian Literature,* 4th rev. and aug. ed., trans. and adapted by William F. Arndt and F. Wilbur Gingrich (Chicago: University of Chicago Press, 1957), pp. 623-624.

[4] Conrad Aiken, "The Return," in *Collected Poems* (New York: Oxford University Press, Inc., 1953, 1970; renewed 1981), as cited in *The New Pocket Anthology of American Verse: From Colonial Days to the Present,* ed. Oscar Williams (New York: Washington Square Press, imprint of Pocket Books, 1955), p. 33.

[5] *Ibid.*

[6] Brown, *The Gospel According to John (xiii-xxi),* vol. 29A, p. 1143.

[7] *Ibid.*, p. 1136.

[8] *Ibid.*

[9] *Ibid.*, p. 1137.

[10] *Ibid.*

[11] Bauer, *op. cit.*, p. 586.

[12] Brown, *The Gospel According to John (xiii-xxi),* vol. 29A, p. 640.

[13] Benjamin Jowett, trans., and Irwin Edman, ed., *The Works of Plato* (New York: Random House, Inc., Modern Library, 1928), p. 188.

[14] Anthony Burgess, *Man of Nazareth* (New York: McGraw-Hill, Inc., 1979), pp. 334-335. Used with the permission of McGraw-Hill Book Company.

[15] Brown, *The Gospel According to John (xiii-xxi),* vol. 29A, p. 646.

[16] *Ibid.*, p. 641.

[17] Excerpts from Raymond E. Brown, trans. and ed., *The Gospel According to John (i-xii),* The Anchor Bible Series (New York: Doubleday & Company, Inc., 1966), vol. 29, p. xcix. Copyright © 1970 by Doubleday & Company, Inc. Reprinted by permission of the publisher.

[18] Brown, *The Gospel According to John (xiii-xxi)*, vol. 29A, p. 641.

[19] *Ibid.*, p. 638.

[20] The sermon is based on John 14:1-23 and Acts 2:1-4 and employs various Bible translations.

[21] Kenneth Cauthen quoting Claude Welch.

[22] Jowett and Edman, *op. cit.*, p. 186.

[23] Matthew Arnold, "Dover Beach," in *The New Oxford Book of English Verse, 1250-1950*, ed. Helen Gardner (New York: Oxford University Press, Inc., 1972), p. 703.